SPECIALTIES
OF THE HOUSE

Specialties OF THE HOUSE

Great Recipes From Great Chicago Restaurants

Chicago House & Social Service Agency, Inc.

Staff

Project Coordinators: William McBride
                         Jim LiSacchi

Project Coordinator,
Design and Production: Mary Schafer

Editorial and Production: Ronald Rutkowski
                         Teri L. Firmiss
                         Marcia Mann
                         Susan Shorey
                         Linda Williams

Book Design: Mary Schafer

Indexes: Nanci Shirrell

Word Processing: Bruce Douglas
                         Paul Henderson

The recipes in this book have been home-tested. Some may differ slightly from similar items served in the restaurants.

Guacamole Picado, Mole Verde con Pachugas de Pollo © 1987 by Rick Bayless and Deann Groen Bayless, by Permission of William Morrow & Company

Library of Congress Cataloging-in-Publication Data

Specialties of the house.

Includes index.
1. Cookery, International. 2. Cookery—Illinois—Chicago. I. Chicago House & Social Service Agency.
TX725.A1S59 1987   641.5'09773'11   87-25000

ISBN 1-55652-026-3

Copyright © 1988 by Chicago House & Social Service Agency, Inc.
801 W. Cornelia #2N, Chicago, Illinois 60657
All rights reserved. Printed in the United States of America

10 9 8 7 6 5 4 3 2 1

To lend a helping hand
in a time of need
Is to strengthen the spirit and
compassion of all humanity.

This book is dedicated to the residents,
employees, volunteers, and supporters
of Chicago House, a not-for-profit
corporation that operates residences
for persons with AIDS.

Acknowledgments

The following individuals and corporations donated materials and services toward the publication of Specialties of the House. Chicago House wishes to extend its sincerest appreciation to all of them for their generosity and concern.

Cover, Illustrations, and Design Production:	McKnight Design
Typesetting:	Typographics – Chicago, IL
Printing:	Malloy Lithographing, Inc.
Paper:	LaSalle Messinger
Distribution:	Independent Publishers Group
Sales:	Fujii Associates, Inc.
Recipe Testing:	Cooking and Hospitality Institute of Chicago
	The Culinary School of Kendall College
	Hospitality Industry–Triton College
	Volunteers from Chicago House
	and nearly 100 other volunteers
Advertising:	*Chicago's Rage*
	Ira T. Johnson
Public Relations:	Laura Manushkin, Creative Ideas Unlimited
Legal Services:	Lawrence Apolzon
Proofreading:	Proof Positive
Color Separation:	Trico Graphics
Template Printing:	Advantage Printers

Chicago House extends special thanks to the following individuals whose assistance made this book possible:

Morris McKnight, Frank Kurland, and Chuck Gonzales of McKnight Design; Chris Preston of Typographics–Chicago, IL; Dick McKee and Dale Taylor, Malloy Lithographing, Inc.; Jim Seeberg, LaSalle Messinger; Curt Mathews, Mark Suchomel, and Amy Teschner of Chicago Review Press; Peter Korth, Avanzare; Janet Connor, Marshall Field's; Leslee Reis, Café Provençal; Gordon Sinclair and Norman Robertson, Gordon; Jeff Smith, The Frugal Gourmet; Bev Bennet, *Chicago Sun-Times;* Carla Kelson, *Chicago Magazine;* Carol Haddix, *Chicago Tribune;* James Ward, WLS-TV; and to all the restaurants who donated their recipes.

Contents

Foreword

I already have over 1000 cookbooks, so it would appear that I don't need any more. Some of the books were given to me in the midst of campaigns to raise funds for this institution or that, this league or that, this movement or that. And most of these "special project books" are filled with molded gelatin salads and cold pasta dishes.

Not so here!

I am terribly proud to be asked to offer a foreword to **Specialties of the House: Great Recipes from Great Chicago Restaurants.** I have two reasons for my pride. The first is the restaurant trade in Chicago.

When I first began visiting Chicago, I was not particularly impressed with the restaurants in the city. What a grand and creative change we have witnessed since then. In only a few years, a very few, Chicago has become one of the great eating cities in America. Oh, we still love hot dogs, ribs, and pizza, but the range of really fine food has gone from our old threesome to every cuisine imaginable. I am proud of the growth, the changes, the taste—and yet the whole works still has the open and supportive flair of Chicago lifestyle. We are willing to try anything, but we Chicagoans (I say that by way of my personal adoption by you people) have proven ourselves to be much more sophisticated in terms of our knowledge of food than anyone on either the West or the East Coast would believe.

Take a look at the table of contents. We have recipes in this book from places that advertise "Coat and Tie Required" and we have recipes from eating houses that offer standing room only. I read through the list and immediately went to my refrigerator. I did not intend to cook. It is just that I found the contributions to this volume to be so attractive, creative, and appetizing that I decided I was hungry. That is the point behind a good recipe, you know. It has nothing to do with whether or not you are really hungry, but rather with the ability of the recipe to excite you. I am excited by these recipes. They represent some of the most creative cooking in America, and they are all Chicago—all of them. Since I eat in most of these places often, I dare not give you my favorites or I will be in serious trouble. Suffice it to say that this is not a "gelatin salad and cold pasta" fund raising book. This is a serious collection of culinary joys, offered—no, given—to us by some truly great cooks.

The second reason that I am proud to offer this foreword stems from the concern that motivated the editors and contributors. This book is an effort at support for Chicago House, a first-class, non-profit agency that offers a residence and support for persons with AIDS. Brillat Savarin said, "The joys of the table belong to all people and for all times." So it is with the offering of comfort to those who suffer from the disease that has become our most recent symbol of alienation and loneliness. All are affected and all must act with compassion, concern, and support.

You will enjoy the recipes in this book and you will enjoy the knowledge that you have helped one or more human beings feel better in the midst of very difficult times.

Jeff Smith

Appetizers

Oysters

Appetizers

Pesce Spada Marinati   (Swordfish Carpaccio)

Juice of 3 lemons
1 swordfish fillet, 12 to 16 ounces,
    cut into 8 very thin slices
½ cup fresh herbs such as basil,
    chives, rosemary, sage,
    and Italian parsley, chopped
    and mixed
1 tablespoon green peppercorns,
    chopped
1 large carrot, sliced julienne
1 large leek, white part only,
    sliced julienne

1 cup extra virgin olive oil
Salt
Freshly ground black pepper
2 tablespoons mascarpone
    cheese
2 tablespoons whipping cream
4 red-leaf lettuce leaves
1 tomato, peeled, seeded, and
    cut into julienne strips

Line a sheet pan with aluminum foil. Pour half of the lemon juice on the pan and spread evenly. Place the swordfish slices on the pan for 15 minutes while cutting the vegetables. Then turn the swordfish over. Top the slices with the herbs, green peppercorns, carrot, and leek. Mix the remaining lemon juice with the olive oil and ladle over each slice. Add salt and pepper to taste.

Whip the mascarpone and whipping cream together until stiff peaks are formed. Place a lettuce leaf on each plate. Arrange the swordfish and tomatoes on the lettuce. Top with a spoonful of the mascarpone-cream mixture.

Serves 4.

AVANZARE
161 E. Huron
Chicago, Illinois 60611
(312) 457-8056

Cajun Crabcakes

12 ounces lump crabmeat, fresh
    or frozen, picked over
1 teaspoon Dijon mustard
1 tablespoon chopped cilantro
½ cup mayonnaise
2 cups fresh breadcrumbs
4 tablespoons unsalted butter

Mix the crabmeat, mustard, cilantro, and mayonnaise together until well blended. Form this mixture into 8 cakes, approximately 1½ inches in diameter. Spread the breadcrumbs on a flat dish or pie plate. Lightly bread each crabcake, coating evenly. Refrigerate the breaded crabcakes for at least ½ hour to set crumbs.

Melt the butter over medium heat in a large skillet. Sauté the crabcakes on each side until golden.

Serves 4.

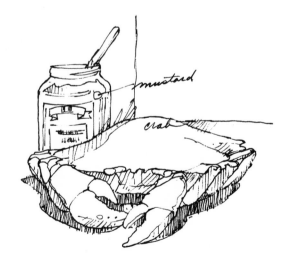

CRICKET'S
100 E. Chestnut Street
Chicago, Illinois 60611
(312) 280-2100

Oysters Copa

2 tablespoons grated horseradish
    (not prepared in cream)
1 cup sour cream
1 teaspoon chopped fresh dill
24 fresh oysters
Crushed ice, spread in a deep,
    metal serving dish
½ ounce lake salmon caviar
½ ounce Hackelback
    sturgeon caviar

Squeeze the excess liquid from the horseradish and add the horseradish
to the sour cream. Add the fresh dill and mix thoroughly. Open the
oysters, rinse, and place them in their shell halves on the crushed ice.
Spoon 2 teaspoons of the sour cream–horseradish mixture over each
oyster. Top 12 of the oysters with the lake salmon caviar, and 12 with the
Hackelback sturgeon caviar.

Note: The sauce can be prepared an hour or two before serving. Cover
the opened oysters with a wet towel and refrigerate. Remove the towel,
then top with the sauce and the caviar just before serving.

Serves 4 to 6.

THE WINNETKA GRILL
64 Green Bay Road
Winnetka, Illinois 60093
(312) 441-6444

Oysters Rockefeller

2 tablespoons unsalted butter
2 tablespoons flour
1 cup hot milk
Nutmeg
Salt
White pepper
1 cup freshly grated imported
    Parmesan cheese

1 cup freshly grated Swiss cheese
Milk
24 oysters on the half shell
1 cup cooked chopped spinach,
    water squeezed out
4 pie tins filled with rock salt

Preheat the oven to 450°.

To prepare the Mornay sauce:
Melt the butter in a heavy saucepan over medium heat. Stir in the flour
and continue to stir constantly until the mixture cooks and bubbles
for about 2 minutes. Do not let the mixture brown. Add the hot milk
gradually, stirring with a whisk as the sauce thickens. Bring to a boil. Add
a pinch of nutmeg, and salt and pepper to taste. Lower the heat. While
still stirring, add the cheeses and cook for about 2 or 3 more minutes.
Remove the sauce from the heat. Float a thin layer of milk on top of the
sauce to prevent a skin from forming. Set aside.

To prepare the oysters:
Clean and shuck each oyster, leaving the oyster in the deep half of the
shell. Place a small dollop of spinach on each oyster. Next, spoon on just
enough Mornay sauce to cover the spinach. Place the oysters on the rock
salt and bake about 6 to 8 minutes, or until the Mornay sauce begins to
turn golden.

Serves 4 to 6.

PHILANDER'S
1120 Pleasant Street
Oak Park, Illinois 60302
(312) 848-4250

Sea Scallops with Mint, Montrechet, and Cappelini

1 pound cappelini (angel hair pasta)
2 cups heavy cream
6 ounces Montrechet cheese
1½ teaspoons coarsely cracked
    black pepper
18 ounces large sea scallops

1½ tablespoons chopped fresh
    mint
1½ tablespoons chopped fresh
    parsley
4 tablespoons unsalted butter

Cook the pasta in a large pot of boiling, salted water. Cappelini will cook very quickly, in about 45 seconds if fresh. Do not overcook. Drain well and chill.

In a large saucepan, gently simmer the cream and Montrechet. Do not boil. Reduce to about 1½ cups. Add the pepper and the scallops. Turn off the heat and cover the pan. The scallops will poach in 1 minute maximum. Check for desired doneness. Add 1 tablespoon of the mint and 1 tablespoon of the parsley and stir.

Melt the butter in another large saucepan and add the drained pasta. Toss with the remaining mint and parsley. Divide the pasta among 6 serving plates.

Bring the sauce to a boil. Add salt to taste and correct consistency of the sauce by reducing or adding a splash of cream. Sauce should be thick enough to coat the back of a spoon. Top the pasta with the sauce and the scallops.

Serves 6.

STAR TOP CAFÉ
2748 N. Lincoln Avenue
Chicago, Illinois 60614
(312) 281-0997

Cajun Barbecued Prawns

½ pound (2 sticks) unsalted butter
½ pound (2 sticks) salted butter
1 tablespoon freshly ground
      black pepper
1 teaspoon white pepper
½ teaspoon cayenne pepper
1 teaspoon paprika
½ teaspoon granulated garlic
16 large shrimp, peeled,
      deveined, and butterflied
Chopped parsley, for garnish
Lemon slices, for garnish

Melt the butter in a skillet over medium heat. Add the black, white, and cayenne peppers, paprika, and garlic. Stir. Sauté the butterflied shrimp in the seasoned butter for about 1 minute on each side. Place 4 shrimp on each of 4 salad plates and pour ¼ of the seasoned butter in the center of each plate. Garnish with lemon slices and parsley.

Serves 4.

BENCHERS FISH HOUSE
Sears Tower
233 S. Wacker Drive
Chicago, Illinois 60606
(312) 993-0096

Louisiana Shrimp with Beans, Tomato, and Basil

1 cup dry white wine
6 cups water
2 medium yellow onions,
    roughly chopped
2 carrots, roughly chopped
4 stalks celery with leaves,
    roughly chopped
4 sprigs parsley
2 bay leaves
¼ teaspoon thyme
¼ teaspoon basil
12 whole black peppercorns
16 large shrimp in their shells

1 cup fresh white beans
    (or dried Great Northerns,
    soaked overnight)
6 to 8 tablespoons fruity extra
    virgin olive oil
3 dried red chili peppers
Salt
Freshly ground black pepper
2 large tomatoes, peeled, seeded,
    and coarsely chopped
¼ cup fresh basil, julienned
Whole basil leaves, for garnish

Make a court bouillon by combining all the ingredients up to and including the peppercorns in a large saucepan. Bring the mixture to a boil, reduce heat, and simmer for half an hour.

While the court bouillon is simmering, peel and devein the shrimp, reserving the shells. Wash the shells thoroughly and add these to the court bouillon. Simmer the shells in the bouillon for 15 minutes. Strain the bouillon through a sieve, pressing the vegetables to extract as much flavor as possible. Return the strained bouillon to the saucepan.

Cook the beans in the bouillon—about 1 hour if using dried beans, 10 to 20 minutes if using fresh. Remove the beans from the bouillon and set them aside, covered.

Heat the oil in a skillet over medium heat. Sauté the peppers in the oil for 3 to 4 minutes, being careful to regulate the heat so the oil doesn't get too hot and the peppers don't burn. When the oil has taken on the spicy quality of the peppers, remove the peppers and discard them. Set the oil aside.

Poach the shrimp in the simmering court bouillon until just done, about 4 to 5 minutes depending on the size of the shrimp. Remove to a plate.

Just before serving, warm the oil gently in a skillet. Add the beans and toss. Adjust the seasoning—you want a sense of pepperiness, but you don't want to overwhelm the other flavors. Add the tomatoes and basil. Add salt and pepper to taste. Divide the bean mixture among 4 serving plates. Top with 4 shrimp each. Garnish with whole basil leaves. Serve warm.

Serves 4.

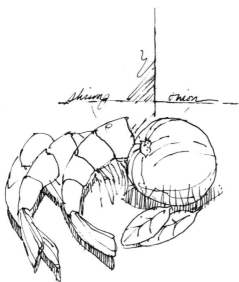

CAFÉ PROVENÇAL
1625 Hinman Avenue
Evanston, Illinois 60201
(312) 475-2233

Shrimp Binyon

30 large shrimp in their shells
¾ pound best-quality white
    bread
2 sticks unsalted butter, softened
2 cloves garlic, minced
2 tablespoons sauterne
½ teaspoon MSG (optional)
½ teaspoon paprika
2 tablespoons dry sherry

Steam the shrimp in their shells until they turn pink. When the shrimp have cooled, peel and devein them.

Preheat the oven to 450 °. Trim the crust from the bread and process the bread into fine crumbs. Cream the butter and combine it with the bread crumbs, garlic, sauterne, and MSG, if desired. Knead the mixture thoroughly as you would bread dough, then roll it into a cylinder about 3 inches in diameter. Refrigerate for an hour.

Divide the cooked shrimp among 6 individual gratin dishes and pour the sherry over them. Slice the butter mixture into ¼-inch slices and lay evenly on top of the shrimp. Sprinkle each serving with paprika and bake in the oven for 8 to 10 minutes or until the butter mixture is a bubbling golden brown.

Serves 6.

BINYON'S
327 S. Plymouth Court
Chicago, Illinois 60604
(312) 341-1155

Crevettes au Chou et Caviar
(Shrimp with Cabbage and Caviar)

5 shrimp (10 to 15 to the pound)
   or 10 baby shrimp, peeled
   and deveined
Salt
White pepper
2 tablespoons unsalted butter,
   divided
1½ cups shredded white cabbage
¾ cup heavy cream
1 teaspoon caviar

Sprinkle the shrimp with salt and pepper. Melt one tablespoon of
the butter in a skillet. When hot, add the shrimp. Sauté over high heat
for about 50 to 60 seconds. With a slotted spoon, transfer the shrimp
to a plate.

Add the cabbage to the juices in the pan and sauté for about 10 seconds.
Add the cream and bring to a boil. Reduce the cabbage and cream
mixture over high heat for a few minutes until the cream coats the spoon.
Add salt and pepper to taste. With a slotted spoon, remove the cabbage
to individual serving dishes. Mix some of the sauce with the cabbage.

Break the remaining tablespoon of butter into small pieces. Add to the
sauce remaining in the skillet. Swirl the sauce in the pan after adding
each piece.

Arrange the shrimp on top of the cabbage. Pour the rest of the sauce over
each serving and sprinkle with caviar. Serve immediately.

Serves 1 to 2.

LE FRANÇAIS
269 S. Milwaukee Avenue
Wheeling, Illinois 60090
(312) 541-7470

Tod Mun Koong *(Deep Fried Shrimp Cakes)*

1 pound medium-sized
    fresh shrimp, peeled
    and deveined
⅛ pound fresh green
    beans, trimmed
1 egg
1 teaspoon red curry paste*
Vegetable oil

Place the shrimp, green beans, egg, and curry paste in a food processor or blender and process into a smooth paste. With wet hands, form the mixture into small balls (walnut sized) and flatten slightly.

Pour 1 inch of oil into a deep skillet and heat to medium. Fry the shrimp cakes for about 1 minute on each side until golden brown. Serve with the cucumber salad (see Chicken Satay, page 16) to which you have added 1 teaspoon ground roasted peanuts and Tabasco sauce to taste.

Serves 6 (18 to 20 cakes).

*Available at Oriental grocery stores.

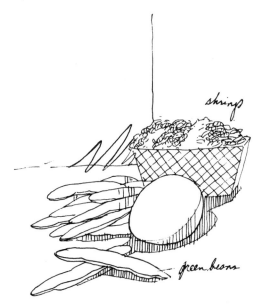

STAR OF SIAM
11 E. Illinois
Chicago, Illinois 60611
(312) 670-0100

Brioche with Snails and Wild Mushrooms

1 pound fresh wild mushrooms
   (shiitake, oyster, morel,
   for example)*
3 tablespoons unsalted butter
2 shallots, minced
36 canned snails
½ cup dry white wine
½ cup snail juice reserved from
   cans

1 cup whipping cream
1 teaspoon freshly snipped chives
Salt
Freshly ground pepper
6 small appetizer-sized brioche**
1 carrot, peeled, finely julienned,
   and blanched

Brush the mushrooms with a damp cloth to remove any dirt or grit. Leave stems on and slice the mushrooms lengthwise. Heat 2 tablespoons of butter over medium heat in a large sauté pan. Sauté the mushrooms until tender and set aside. Sauté the shallots in the remaining tablespoon of butter. Add the snails and stir. Add the white wine and the reserved snail juice, stirring constantly. Simmer for 5 minutes and then remove the snails.

Turn the heat up to high and reduce the liquid to about 1 tablespoon. Add the cream while stirring constantly and reduce by one third. Add the sautéed mushrooms, chives, and cooked snails. Heat through. Season to taste with salt and pepper. Serve on top and around the brioche. Garnish each serving with some julienne of carrot.

Serves 6.

*If fresh wild mushrooms are unavailable, fresh domestic mushrooms can be used.

**Available fresh from bakeries or frozen from supermarkets.

LE TITI DE PARIS
1015 W. Dundee Road
Arlington Heights, Illinois 60004
(312) 506-0222

Escargots Florentine

1 teaspoon unsalted butter
12 canned snails, washed
2 cups (firmly packed) fresh
   spinach, well rinsed
   and stemmed
Freshly ground black pepper

2 ounces bleu cheese, crumbled
2 tablespoons heavy cream
2 teaspoons freshly grated
   imported Parmesan or
   Romano cheese
Lemon wedges, for garnish

Melt the butter in a sauté pan over medium heat. Add the snails and the spinach. Add the black pepper to taste. Sauté over medium heat for about 3 to 4 minutes until the spinach begins to wilt. Add the bleu cheese. Reduce the heat and simmer for about 4 to 6 minutes until the cheese is melted. Add the cream and mix well.

Transfer the mixture to 2 individual gratin dishes or ramekins. Sprinkle the grated Parmesan or Romano cheese on top and place under the broiler for about 2 to 3 minutes until the cheese is lightly browned. Garnish with lemon wedges. Serve immediately.

Serves 2.

bleu cheese

escargot

R.S.V.P. & CO.
3324 N. Broadway
Chicago, Illinois 60657
(312) 975-1102

Escargots of the Manor

5 tablespoons unsalted butter
3 tablespoons flour
4 shallots, minced
1 cup chablis
2 cups fish stock or bottled clam
        juice
1 cup heavy cream
24 imported large French snails
½ clove garlic, minced
½ pound fresh spinach pasta
Parsley, for garnish
Lemon twists, for garnish

In a heavy saucepan, make a roux by first melting 3 tablespoons of the butter over medium heat. When foam subsides, add the 3 tablespoons of flour and cook, stirring constantly with a wooden spoon, for 2 to 3 minutes. Do not let roux darken.

In a medium saucepan, simmer the shallots and wine until reduced by half. Add the fish stock or clam juice and the heavy cream. Bring to a full boil. Add the roux and simmer for 5 minutes.

In a sauté pan, melt the remaining 2 tablespoons of butter over medium heat. Add the snails and minced garlic. Sauté for 1 minute. Add the cream sauce and simmer for an additional minute.

Cook the pasta in a large pot of boiling, salted water until *al dente*. Drain well, and add to the snails and warm through. With a forked serving spoon, roll the pasta into the shape of a bird's nest and place in the middle of each plate. Place 6 snails in the middle of each nest. Garnish with a sprig of parsley and a twist of lemon.

Serves 4.

ASH MANOR
1600 Diversey Parkway
Chicago, Illinois 60614
(312) 248-1600

Chicken Satay (Thai Shish Kebab)

For the peanut sauce:
1 cup Thai coconut milk*
1 teaspoon red curry paste*
2 tablespoons sugar
½ teaspoon salt
¼ cup hot water
8 ounces creamy peanut butter

For the cucumber salad:
¼ cup hot water
¼ cup distilled white vinegar
¼ teaspoon salt

1 tablespoon sugar
2 cucumbers, thinly sliced
Several thin onion slices
4 slices fresh hot red chili pepper

For the satay:
1 pound boneless chicken breast
1 teaspoon curry powder
¼ teaspoon salt
¾ tablespoon sugar
½ cup Thai coconut milk
12 bamboo skewers, soaked

To prepare the peanut sauce:
Bring the coconut milk to a boil in a medium saucepan. Reduce the heat. Add the curry paste, sugar, and salt. Return the mixture to a boil, stirring frequently. Add the hot water and peanut butter, stirring until all the ingredients are blended. Do not scorch.

To prepare the cucumber salad:
Bring the hot water, vinegar, salt, and sugar to a boil in a small saucepan. Let the mixture cool. Pour this dressing over the sliced cucumbers in a bowl and top with the onion and chili pepper slices.

To prepare the satay:
Preheat the oven to 550°. Pound the chicken until it is about ¼ inch thick. Cut it into 1-inch squares. Marinate it in the curry powder, salt, sugar, and about ½ cup of the coconut milk for at least 30 minutes in the refrigerator. Thread the chicken onto the skewers. Bake on a cookie sheet. Check after 3 minutes for doneness. Do not overcook. (Chicken can also be cooked on a charcoal grill.) Serve with the salad and the peanut sauce.

Serves 6.

*Available at Oriental grocery stores.

STAR OF SIAM
11 E. Illinois
Chicago, Illinois 60611
(312) 670-0100

Smoked Chicken Hush Puppies

1 cup yellow cornmeal
¾ cup flour
1 tablespoon baking powder
1 tablespoon sugar
½ teaspoon salt
Pinch of cayenne pepper
Meat from 1 small smoked
    chicken, chopped,
    or 1½ pounds smoked
    turkey, chopped

2 eggs
½ to ¾ cup buttermilk
½ cup chopped green
    bell pepper
½ cup chopped scallions
3 cups vegetable shortening or
    vegetable oil

Mix together the first 7 ingredients. Add the eggs, buttermilk, pepper, and scallions. Form the mixture into balls about the size of a walnut.

Heat the shortening or oil to 360°. Spoon the hush puppy balls a few at a time into the oil. Fry until golden. Serve with cocktail sauce or sour cream.

Makes about 18 hush puppies.

CORNELIA'S
750 W. Cornelia
Chicago, Illinois 60657
(312) 248-8333

Saganaki *(Flaming Greek Cheese)*

½ cup milk
1 egg
¼ pound kaseri cheese, cut into
      ½-inch thick slices*
Flour for dredging
Olive oil
Brandy
4 lemon halves

Beat the milk and egg together (batter is sufficient for 4 to 5 slices of cheese). Prepare 1 slice of cheese at a time by dipping it in the milk-egg mixture, then in the flour. Refrigerate for 1 to 3 hours.

Pour about ¼ inch of the olive oil into a frying pan. Heat the oil over medium heat. Brown the cheese slices on each side in the hot oil. Remove the slices and place them on heated metal steak plates or in individual frying pans. Pour ½ ounce of brandy over each slice of cheese. Flame. Douse the flames by squeezing the juice from the lemon halves over the cheese. Serve immediately.

Serves 4 to 5.

*Available at Greek grocery stores.

COURTYARDS OF PLAKA
340 S. Halsted
Chicago, Illinois 60606
(312) 263-0767

Pizza with Mushrooms, Pancetta, Pine Nuts, Goat Cheese and Rosemary

1 tablespoon dried yeast, inactive
1/2 cup water at 110°
1 teaspoon salt
3 cups all-purpose flour
1 cup whole wheat flour
1/2 teaspoon baking powder
2 tablespoons olive oil
1 cup plus 1 teaspoon water
2 ounces pancetta*

1/4 cup red onion, diced
1 ounce oyster mushrooms, sliced
1 ounce pine nuts
1/2 cup goat cheese
8 sprigs rosemary, blanched
2 ounces shredded mozzarella
   cheese

To prepare the whole wheat crust:
Dissolve the yeast with the water. Let stand for 10 minutes. In a large mixing bowl, combine the salt, flours, baking powder, and olive oil. Add the yeast-water mixture and the 1 cup plus 1 teaspoon of water. With a hook attachment on a mixer, or in a food processor, knead the dough until it forms a ball. Place the dough into an oiled bowl. Cover. Let the dough rise until it doubles in size. Punch down the dough and let it rise again in the refrigerator. Cover as before. Roll out the dough into 2 pizza crusts.

To prepare the topping:
Preheat the oven to 500°. Spread the pancetta, red onion, mushrooms, and pine nuts over the pizza crusts. Add the goat cheese in dabs to the four corners. Sprinkle with the rosemary leaves. Cover lightly with the mozzarella. Bake 8 to 10 minutes on a preheated ceramic stone or a cornmeal-sprinkled cookie sheet. Serve immediately.

*Available at Italian or specialty grocery stores.

FOLEY'S ON OHIO
211 E. Ohio
Chicago, Illinois 60601
(312) 645-1261

Alcachofas con Jamon
(Sautéed Artichokes with Ham)

6 medium artichokes
Juice of 1 lemon
½ cup white vinegar
Salt
¼ cup olive oil
2 teaspoons minced garlic
2 medium tomatoes, peeled,
    seeded, and diced

4 ounces ham, serrano or
    prosciutto, cut into
    ½-inch cubes
Freshly ground black pepper
2 tablespoons chopped fresh
    parsley

Snip the prickly tips off the artichoke leaves with scissors. Cut off the tips of the stems. Rub the stems of the artichokes with the lemon juice to prevent discoloring. Place the artichokes in a large pot. Add the vinegar, salt to taste, and enough cold water to cover. Boil gently for about 30 minutes until fork-tender. (Artichokes may also be steamed.) Drain and cool. Remove the leaves and peel the stems. Use a teaspoon to scoop out and remove the fuzzy chokes, leaving the bottoms and stems. Cut each artichoke bottom lengthwise into quarters.

Heat the olive oil in a large sauté pan. Add the garlic and sauté for 1 to 2 minutes. Add the artichokes, tomatoes, and ham. Cook over medium heat until everything is hot. Divide into 4 cazuelas (clay dishes) or onto 4 plates. Season with salt and pepper to taste. Sprinkle with parsley and serve immediately.

Serves 4.

CAFÉ BA-BA-REEBA!
2024 N. Halsted
Chicago, Illinois 60614
(312) 935-5000

Guacamole Picado *(Avocado Relish)*

½ small onion, very
    finely chopped
Fresh hot green chiles to taste
    (roughly 2 chiles serranos
    or 1 chile jalapeño,
    stemmed, seeded, and
    very finely chopped)*
1 ripe, medium-large tomato,
    cored and very finely
    chopped (optional)
1 clove garlic, peeled and very
    finely chopped (optional)

10 sprigs fresh coriander
    (cilantro), chopped (optional)
3 ripe, medium avocados
Salt, about ½ teaspoon
½ lime, juiced (optional)
Additional chopped onion and
    fresh coriander, radish slices
    or roses, and/or a little
    crumbled Mexican queso
    fresco or other fresh cheese
    like feta or farmer's cheese,
    for garnish

In a medium-sized bowl, mix the finely chopped onion and *chiles* with the optional tomato, garlic, and coriander.

Close to the time you are going to serve, halve the avocados lengthwise by cutting from the stem to flower ends, around the pits. Twist the avocado halves in opposite directions to loosen the meat from the pits, then scoop out the pits and reserve. Scrape the avocado pulp from the skins and add it to the bowl.

Using your hand or a spoon, roughly mash the avocado while mixing in the other ingredients, making a coarse, thick mass. Flavor with salt, then enough lime juice to add a little zing, if you wish. Return the pits to the guacamole and cover with a sheet of plastic wrap pressed directly onto the surface of the mixture. Set aside for a few minutes to let the flavors blend.

The guacamole is very attractive in a pottery bowl or Mexican mortar, sprinkled with chopped onion, coriander, radish slices, and crumbled fresh cheese.

Serves 6.

*Available at Mexican grocery stores.

FRONTERA GRILL
445 N. Clark
Chicago, Illinois 60610
(312) 661-1434

Papas Rellenas *(Peruvian Stuffed Potatoes)*

For the potatoes:
1 ½ pounds peeled Idaho potatoes
½ teaspoon salt
½ teaspoon freshly ground
    black pepper

For the filling:
2 tablespoons lard or
    vegetable oil
¾ pound ground beef
2 cloves garlic, crushed
¾ cup chopped onion
½ teaspoon salt
¼ teaspoon freshly
    ground pepper
¼ teaspoon ground oregano
2 hard-boiled eggs, chopped

⅓ cup seedless raisins
¼ cup pitted, chopped
    Greek olives
2 teaspoons chopped parsley

For the salsa:
1 cup chopped onion
Juice of 2 lemons
Salt
4 teaspoons hot oil, or more or
    less to taste*
Cilantro leaves

Flour for dredging
1 egg, slightly beaten
32 ounces vegetable oil
Cilantro leaves, for garnish
Lemon wedges, for garnish

Note: This recipe is easier to prepare if the ingredients are cooked and refrigerated the day before you plan to serve the potatoes.

To prepare the potatoes:
Place the potatoes in a large pot and cover with water; boil until tender. Cool the potatoes, then rice or mash them in a large bowl. Stir in the salt and pepper. On a lightly floured board, knead the potato mixture about 20 turns until it is the consistency of biscuit dough. Shape the potato mixture into a roll about 14 inches long. Wrap in plastic and refrigerate, overnight if possible.

To prepare the filling:
In a large skillet, melt the lard or vegetable oil over medium heat. Add the beef and garlic. Cook until the beef loses its pink color, stirring frequently. Add the onion, salt, pepper, and oregano. Cook until the onion is translucent, about 7 minutes. Add the eggs, raisins, olives, and parsley, and cook for 1 minute, stirring constantly. Allow the filling to become completely cool, or refrigerate until well chilled.

To prepare the salsa:
In a small bowl, combine the onion, lemon juice, and the salt and hot oil to taste. Let marinate several hours or overnite in the refrigerator. Before serving, allow the salsa to come to room temperature. Sprinkle with cilantro leaves.

To assemble the potatoes:
Cut the potato mixture into pieces about 2 to 3 inches thick. Flatten a piece of the mixture in one hand and make a hollow or well in it. Fill the well with several tablespoons of the meat mixture. Shape the potato mixture aroung the filling, forming a potato shape. Dredge the potato in the flour. Pour the oil into a wok or deep skillet and heat until it is hot but not smoking. Dip the potato into the beaten egg to seal it completely. Carefully slide the potato into the oil. As the potato fries, prick frequently with a skewer or a long-tined fork to release the steam. Cook until the potato is golden brown. Repeat the procedure until all the potato mixture is used. Serve at once with the salsa, lemon wedges, and cilantro.

*Available at Oriental grocery stores.

Serves 6 to 8.

LA LLAMA
3811 N. Ashland Avenue
Chicago, Illinois 60613
(312) 327-7756

Kaddo Borawni   (Pan-Fried Baby Pumpkin)

1 baby pumpkin (butternut
    or acorn squash may
    be substituted)
Vegetable oil
2 tablespoons water
½ cup sugar
1½ cups plain yogurt
½ teaspoon garlic powder
½ teaspoon salt
Vegetable oil

2 large onions, diced
1 pound ground beef
1 teaspoon salt
1 teaspoon garlic powder
1 teaspoon black pepper
1 teaspoon ground coriander
¼ teaspoon red pepper flakes
¼ teaspoon turmeric
1 cup tomato sauce

To prepare the pumpkin:
Slice the pumpkin in half. Remove the seeds. Cut the pumpkin meat into
2 x 3-inch squares, each 1 inch thick. Peel each square. Heat the oil in a
skillet over low heat. Add the pumpkin, water, and sugar, and cover the
skillet. When the water begins to boil, turn up the heat to medium; the
oil will come to the surface. The pumpkin is cooked when tender, about
15 to 20 minutes.

To prepare the yogurt sauce:
Mix 1½ cups plain yogurt with ½ teaspoon garlic powder and
½ teaspoon salt.

To prepare the meat sauce:
Heat the oil in a large skillet and sauté the onions until translucent. Add
the ground beef and sauté until browned. Add all the spices and stir.
Add the tomato sauce and cook for 5 minutes.

To serve, place 3 tablespoons of the yogurt sauce on each of 6 plates.
Divide the pumpkin into 6 equal portions and arrange on the yogurt.
Crisscross 1 teaspoon of yogurt sauce on top of the pumpkin. Surround
the pumpkin with approximately 4 tablespoons of meat sauce.
Serve immediately.

Serves 6.

THE HELMAND
3201 N. Halsted
Chicago, Illinois 60657
(312) 935-2447

Wild Mushrooms Provençal

2 large tomatoes, peeled, seeded,
    and chopped
1 small yellow onion, finely
    minced
1 small whole garlic clove, peeled
1 bay leaf
½ cup dry white wine or dry
    vermouth
Thyme
12 ounces of fresh, wild
    mushrooms (trumpet,
    shiitake, oyster, for example)
1 stick unsalted butter
1 clove garlic, minced
1 tablespoon minced fresh parsley
Salt
Pepper

Begin by making the Provençal sauce. Combine the tomatoes, onion, garlic, bay leaf, white wine, and a pinch of thyme in a saucepan. Bring to a boil. Then reduce heat and simmer for 35 minutes, stirring frequently.

While the sauce is cooking, brush the mushrooms lightly with a damp cloth to remove any grit. Do not wash the mushrooms. Slice the mushrooms lengthwise, leaving the stems on. Heat the butter over medium heat in a sauté pan. Add the garlic and parsley and sauté for 1 to 2 minutes. Then add the sliced mushrooms and turn up the heat to high. Sauté over high heat until tender. Season with salt and pepper to taste. Place on a serving plate and garnish with Provençal sauce.

Serves 4.

LA BOHÈME
566 Chestnut Street
Winnetka, Illinois 60093
(312) 446-4600

Soups

Asparagus Crab Soup

2 cans white asparagus spears,
    15 ounces each
6 cups chicken stock, preferably
    homemade
½ pound cooked Alaskan king
    crab meat, shredded
2 teaspoons salt
4 teaspoons sugar
2 eggs
3 tablespoons cornstarch
Sesame oil
Freshly ground black pepper

Cut the asparagus spears into 1-inch lengths. Pour the chicken stock into a soup pot. Add the asparagus and the shredded crab. Bring the stock to a boil, then reduce the heat until the soup is simmering. Add the salt and sugar.

Break the eggs into a small bowl and beat them lightly. Add the eggs to the soup, stirring as you add them. Continue simmering.

Mix the cornstarch with enough cold water to make a thin paste. Stir this paste into the soup. Simmer until the soup thickens. Spoon the soup into small bowls. Add a few drops of sesame oil and a few grindings of black pepper to each.

Serves 6.

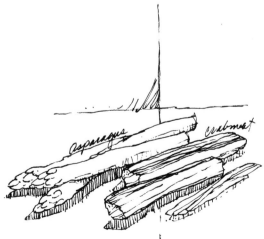

HUÉ
1138 W. Argyle
Chicago, Illinois 60640
(312) 275-4044

Bookbinder Red Snapper Soup

For the soup base:
1 tablespoon clarified butter
1 tablespoon diced carrot
1 tablespoon diced celery
2 tablespoons diced onion
1 small clove garlic, crushed
½ bay leaf
8 white peppercorns, crushed
Thyme
3 tablespoons tomato paste
2 quarts fish stock
4 tablespoons unsalted butter

4 tablespoons flour
2 drops caramel color
Salt

To complete the soup:
1 tablespoon clarified butter
¾ cup diced onion
3 tablespoons diced celery
10 ounces red snapper fillet,
    boned and diced
4 tablespoons California sherry

To prepare the soup base:
In a large soup pot, heat the clarified butter over medium heat and
sauté the carrot, celery, and onion until tender. Add the garlic, bay leaf,
peppercorns, a dash of thyme, and the tomato paste. Cook over medium
heat for a few minutes. Add the fish stock and bring to a boil.

In a separate saucepan, melt the 4 tablespoons of butter over medium
heat. When the butter stops foaming, add the flour and cook, stirring
constantly, for 2 minutes. Stir this mixture into the soup and simmer for
20 minutes. Add the caramel coloring. Season with salt to taste and strain.

To complete the soup:
In a separate saucepan, heat the clarified butter over medium heat. Sauté
the onion and celery. Add the red snapper and the sherry. Sauté for 2 to
3 minutes. Add to the soup base. Heat through and serve immediately.

Serves 8.

CAPE COD ROOM
140 E. Walton
Chicago, Illinois 60611
(312) 787-2200

Mulligatawny Soup

1½ cups coarsely chopped yellow onion

8 tablespoons unsalted butter

2 cloves garlic, thinly sliced

1 rib celery with leaves, coarsely chopped

1 pound carrots, peeled and cut into 1-inch pieces

9 cups chicken broth, preferably homemade

1 teaspoon madras curry powder*

½ teaspoon salt

½ teaspoon white pepper

Cilantro, chopped, for garnish

In a 6-quart pot with a lid, sauté ½ cup of the chopped onions in 4 tablespoons of butter over medium heat until the onions are golden brown. Add the garlic and sauté a minute longer. Add the celery and carrots and sauté briefly. Add the chicken broth and bring to a boil for 2 minutes. Lower heat, cover, and simmer for 45 minutes or until the carrots are tender.

Meanwhile, in a skillet over medium heat, sauté the remaining onions in the remaining 4 tablespoons of butter until the onions are lightly colored. Add the curry powder and sauté another minute, stirring well to blend the flavors. Remove from heat. When the soup is cooked, add the sautéed onions to the soup pot, including any liquid from the onions and butter. Mix the soup well, raise the heat, and bring the soup to a boil. Remove from heat. Purée the hot soup in a blender or food processor until smooth and creamy. Add salt and white pepper to taste. You may pass the soup through a fine sieve. The soup should have the consistency of slightly thickened heavy cream. You may thin the soup by adding hot chicken broth or light cream. Garnish each serving with some chopped cilantro.

Serves 8 to 10.

*Available at Indian grocery stores.

CASBAH
514 W. Diversey
Chicago, Illinois 60614
(312) 935-7570

Tom Ka Gai (Chicken Coconut Milk Soup)

1¾ cups hot water
2 thin slices dried galanga root*
4 pieces lemon grass
    (1 inch long)*
2 bitter lemon leaves (optional)*
½ pound boneless chicken
    breast, cut into chunks
2 ounces cabbage, shredded
1 can (13 to 14 ounces)
    Thai coconut milk
    (not Hawaiian)*

1½ tablespoons sugar
⅓ cup nampla (fish sauce)*
⅓ cup freshly squeezed
    lemon juice
1 tablespoon sliced scallions
1 tablespoon chopped
    fresh cilanto
2 hot red chili peppers, sliced
    thinly (optional)

In a large pot, bring the water, galanga root, lemon grass, and lemon leaves to a boil. Add the chicken breast and simmer about 8 to 10 minutes until done. Skim the foam from the pot. Add the cabbage and boil until tender. Add the coconut milk, sugar, fish sauce, and lemon juice. Simmer for 5 to 10 minutes. Ladle into soup bowls and sprinkle with the scallions, cilantro, and, if desired, the chili peppers. Serve hot.

Serves 6.

*Available at Oriental grocery stores.

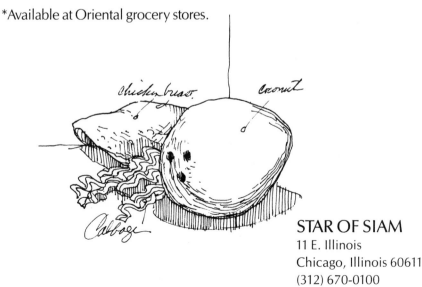

STAR OF SIAM
11 E. Illinois
Chicago, Illinois 60611
(312) 670-0100

Sopa de Tortilla Horneada   (Tortilla Soup)

1 cup vegetable oil
12 corn tortillas, cut into strips
½ cup fresh tomato sauce
6 cups hot chicken broth,
        preferably homemade
6 thin slices Chihuahua cheese
        (or Swiss cheese)*
6 chipotle peppers (or any other
        hot pepper)*

Preheat the oven to 350°.

In a skillet, heat the oil over medium heat and fry the tortilla strips until brown and crispy. Drain them on paper towels.

In a large pot, heat the tomato sauce and chicken broth. Divide the tortilla strips among 6 ovenproof soup bowls. Pour the tomato-chicken broth over the tortilla strips. Place a slice of cheese on top of each bowl and bake for approximately 5 minutes. Garnish the soup with peppers and serve hot.

Serves 6.

*Chihuahua cheese and chipotle peppers are available at Mexican grocery stores.

LAS MAÑANITAS
3523 N. Halsted
Chicago, Illinois 60657
(312) 528-2109

Caribbean Black Bean Soup

2 pounds black beans
1 to 2 tablespoons peanut oil
1 medium yellow onion, diced
4 strips uncooked bacon,
    finely diced
4 cloves garlic, crushed

1 quart chicken stock,
    preferably homemade
1 to 2 tablespoons chopped
    fresh cilantro
Salt
Cayenne pepper

Sort the beans to remove any bad ones. Cover the remaining beans with water in a large pot. Soak for 24 hours.

Heat the peanut oil in a large soup pot. Add the onion and bacon and sauté over medium heat until the onion is translucent. Add the garlic and sauté for another minute. Add the chicken stock, cilantro, and soaked black beans. Cook until the beans are tender, about 1½ hours. Purée half of the soup in a food processor or blender. Return the purée to the remaining soup. Season with salt and cayenne pepper to taste.

Serves 8 to 9.

CRICKET'S
100 E. Chestnut Street
Chicago, Illinois 60611
(312) 280-2100

Lentil Soup

12 ounces lentil beans
3 tablespoons unsalted butter
2 ounces bacon, finely diced
2 ounces shallots, minced
1 teaspoon tomato paste
1 tablespoon vinegar
Salt
White pepper
Marjoram

1 clove garlic, halved
1 quart beef or chicken stock,
    preferably homemade
1 tablespoon diced celery
1 tablespoon diced carrot
1 tablespoon diced leek
2 tablespoons unsalted butter
Parsley or chives, chopped, for
    garnish

Soak the lentils in water overnight. Drain.

Rub the bottom of a large cooking pot with the cut sides of the garlic. Heat the butter over medium heat until the butter foams. Sauté the bacon and shallots until soft. Add the tomato paste and continue to sauté. Stir in the vinegar. Add the drained lentils. Season with the salt, white pepper, and marjoram to taste. Fill the pot with the beef or chicken stock and bring to a boil. Reduce heat to simmer. While the soup is simmering, add the celery, carrots, and leeks. Continue to simmer until the lentils are soft and the vegetables are tender. Strain the lentils from the broth. Pour the broth into a blender, add 2 tablespoons of butter, and blend until smooth. Pour the broth over the still hot lentils. Ladle into soup bowls and garnish each serving with the parsley or chives.

Serves 6.

DIETERLE'S
550 S. McLean Boulevard
Elgin, Illinois 60123
(312) 697-7311

Canadian Cheese Soup

1 tablespoon minced onion
4 tablespoons butter, melted
½ cup flour
1 tablespoon cornstarch
⅛ teaspoon paprika
⅛ teaspoon baking soda
3 cups hot milk
3 cups hot chicken stock,
    preferably homemade
8 cups grated sharp
    cheddar cheese
½ cup carrots, diced and cooked
    until tender
½ cup celery, diced and cooked
    until tender
2 drops Angostura bitters
Salt
1 tablespoon parsley, minced

Sauté the onion in butter until translucent. Do not brown. Mix together the flour, cornstarch, paprika, and baking soda. Add to the onion and butter. Stir over medium heat for 2 minutes to cook the flour. Add the hot milk and the hot chicken stock, stirring constantly. Heat to piping hot, but do not boil. Gradually add the cheese to the soup and stir until melted. Add the carrots, celery, bitters, and salt to taste. Ladle into serving bowls and sprinkle with parsley.

Serves 4 to 6.

THE WALNUT ROOM
Marshall Field's
111 N. State Street
Chicago, Illinois 60602
(312) 781-1000

Sweet and Sour Cabbage Soup

1 tablespoon vegetable oil
½ pound beef brisket, cut into
    ½-inch cubes
2½ quarts water
1½ ounces beef bouillon cubes
1¼ pounds cabbage, cored
    and shredded
1 can (12 ounces) peeled,
    crushed tomatoes
½ cup diced onion
1 teaspoon garlic powder
¾ cup brown sugar,
    firmly packed
¼ cup freshly squeezed
    lemon juice
Freshly ground black pepper
6 tablespoons tomato paste
Lemon slices, for garnish

Heat the oil in a skillet over medium-high heat. Sauté the beef until medium-rare.

In a large soup pot, combine the water, beef bouillon cubes, cabbage, and tomatoes. Bring to a boil. Add the onion, garlic powder, brown sugar, lemon juice, a pinch of pepper, the tomato paste, and the sautéed beef. Simmer for 45 minutes. Serve hot, garnished with lemon slices.

Serves 6 to 8.

MRS. LEVY'S DELICATESSEN
Sears Tower
233 S. Wacker Drive
Chicago, Illinois 60606
(312) 993-0530

Corn Chowder

5 tablespoons unsalted butter
2 red bell peppers, cored, seeded,
    and cut into ¼-inch dice
½ cup sliced wild mushrooms
    (shiitake and oyster,
    for example)
6 scallions, sliced into ¼-inch
    lengths
Kernels cut from 8 medium ears
    of fresh corn
2 tomatoes, peeled, seeded,
    and diced
8 cups chicken stock, preferably
    homemade
Salt
Freshly ground pepper
Chopped fresh herbs of your
    choice (parsley, tarragon,
    or chives, for example)

Melt the butter in a skillet. Add the peppers, wild mushrooms, and
scallions and sauté until tender. Add the corn, cover, and simmer until
tender. In a large soup pot, combine the sautéed ingredients with the
tomatoes and the chicken stock. Bring to a boil and simmer until reduced
by ⅓ to ½. Coarsely purée half of the soup, a cup at a time. Combine
this purée with the remaining soup. Reduce further if desired. Season to
taste with the salt, pepper, and herbs.

Serves 4.

MÉLANGE
1515 N. Sheridan Road
Wilmette, Illinois 60091
(312) 256-1700

Crème Glacé d' Aubergines

(Chilled Cream of Eggplant Soup)

4 ounces (1 stick) unsalted butter
½ pound eggplant, peeled
    and diced
1½ cups chopped yellow onion
1 cup diced celery
1 tablespoon curry powder
½ cup chopped fresh basil
1 pound potatoes, sliced
1½ quarts chicken stock,
preferably homemade
1 cup heavy cream
Salt
Pepper

Melt the butter in a soup pot. Sauté the eggplant, onion, and celery until softened. Add the curry powder and basil and sauté 2 minutes more. Add the potatoes, stirring constantly for another 2 minutes.

Add the chicken stock and cook over medium heat for 15 minutes. Chill in the refrigerator. Before serving, thin to desired consistency with heavy cream. Add salt and pepper to taste.

Serves 6.

L'ESCARGOT
2925 N. Halsted
Chicago, Illinois 60657
(312) 525-5522

Garlic Soup with Shiitake Mushrooms

1½ sticks unsalted butter
1 medium yellow onion, chopped
4 shallots, chopped
Cloves from 4 medium heads
    garlic, peeled and trimmed
    but left whole
4 sprigs thyme
1 pound shiitake mushrooms,
    sliced thin, stems reserved
½ pound white mushrooms,
    sliced
1 cup brandy
4 cups water
2 quarts heavy cream
Salt

Melt the butter in a heavy saucepan. Add the onion, shallots, garlic, thyme, shiitake stems, and white mushrooms. Sauté over medium heat for about 1 hour, stirring frequently. Raise the heat. Add the brandy and let boil for 30 seconds. Then add the water and bring to a simmer. Add the heavy cream slowly, stirring it in. Simmer for about 20 minutes or longer if you prefer a thicker soup. Strain the soup and add the sliced shiitake caps. Add salt to taste and serve.

Serves 10.

GORDON
500 N. Clark Street
Chicago, Illinois 60610
(312) 467-9780

Potato, Leek, and Pepperoni Soup

3 tablespoons unsalted butter
1 large yellow onion, diced
1 large leek, trimmed, washed,
    and sliced into rounds
    (white and green parts)
4 ounces pepperoni, cut into
    1/8-inch slices
2 bay leaves
4 cups chicken stock, preferably
    homemade
2 large red potatoes, scrubbed
    and cut into 1/2-inch cubes
1 cup half-and-half or milk
Salt

Melt the butter in a 4-quart saucepan. Add the onion and leek and sauté, covered, until translucent. Add the pepperoni and bay leaves and cook, covered, 2 to 3 minutes longer.

Add the chicken stock. Bring the mixture to a simmer and then add the potatoes. Continue simmering until the potatoes are tender but still hold their shape. Remove the pan from the heat and skim off any fat from the pepperoni. Stir in the half-and-half or milk. Return the pan to the heat and bring to serving temperature without letting the soup boil. Season with salt to taste before serving.

Serves 4.

WICKLINE'S
3335 N. Halsted
Chicago, Illinois 60657
(312) 525-4415

Tomatillo Gazpacho

2 ½ pounds tomatillos*
2 medium cucumbers, peeled,
    seeded, and cut into 1-inch
    strips
1 small onion, diced
2 large stalks celery, cut into
    ½-inch pieces

24 ounces bottled clam juice
Juice of 1 lime
1 small bunch fresh cilantro
1 red bell pepper, sliced julienne
1 yellow bell pepper, sliced
    julienne

Wash the tomatillos in warm water and remove the husks. Cut out the core and score the bottoms with a knife. Blanch until the skins start to tear. Then plunge the tomatillos into ice water. Carefully peel off the skins and discard. Separate the meat from the seed sacks and keep both, but separated.

Lightly salt the cucumbers and let them drain. Strain the seed sacks of the tomatillos through a sieve until as much juice as possible is extracted. Save the juice and pulp but discard the seeds.

In a blender, purée the onion, tomatillos (meat and juice), celery, and cucumbers with the clam and lime juices. Finely chop two teaspoons of cilantro and add it to the blended soup mixture. Reserve some whole cilantro leaves for the garnish. Sprinkle the peppers on the top of the soup. Refrigerate the soup for several hours. Garnish with whole cilantro leaves before serving.

Note: For a richer flavor, prepare the soup the day before you plan to serve it.

Serves 10.

*Available at Mexican grocery stores.

PRINTER'S ROW
550 S. Dearborn
Chicago, Illinois 60605
(312) 461-0780

Salads

Insalata di Mare   (Seafood Salad)

1 pound fresh Spanish baby
   octopus, cleaned*
1 pound fresh sepia (cuttlefish),
   cleaned*
1 pound fresh calamari (squid),
   cleaned*
1 pound fresh mussels, soaked
   and scrubbed
2 stalks celery, chopped into
   large pieces
2 tablespoons dried oregano
2 tablespoons chopped
   fresh parsley

2 cloves garlic, chopped
12 green Greek olives (optional),
   chopped
1 tablespoon salt
1 teaspoon freshly ground
   black pepper
3 cups virgin olive oil
1 cup white wine vinegar
6 to 8 leaves romaine lettuce
6 to 8 lemon slices, for garnish

Rinse the seafood in cold water. In separate pots of boiling water, cook the octopus, fish, and squid for about 15 to 20 minutes or until tender. Steam the mussels in a separate pot. Chop the octopus into bite-sized pieces. Cut the sepia into thick strips. Cut the calamari into rings. Remove the mussels from their shells. (Use only those mussels from opened shells.)

Mix all the remaining ingredients except the lettuce and lemon slices to make a marinade. Place the seafood in a large bowl and cover with the marinade. Refrigerate overnight, stirring occasionally.

To serve, place a leaf of romaine on each chilled salad plate. Arrange the seafood salad on top. Garnish with slices of lemon.

Serves 6 to 8.

*Available (cleaned and ready to cook) at specialty fish markets.

FRICANO'S
2512 N. Halsted
Chicago, Illinois 60614
(312) 929-7550

Scallop Berry Salad

2 bunches watercress
2 Belgian endives
1 cantaloupe
12 strawberries
½ pint raspberries
½ pint blueberries
2 kiwi fruit
2 cups dry white wine
½ pound sea scallops
½ pound bay scallops

2 whole eggs
2 egg yolks
¼ cup fresh lemon juice
⅛ cup white wine vinegar
¼ cup frozen orange juice
    concentrate
2 teaspoons salt
2 cups peanut oil
Half-and-half

Rinse and drain the watercress and Belgian endives and arrange them on four plates. Wash and prepare the fruit and arrange it on the greens.

Bring the white wine to a boil in a saucepan. Remove it from the heat. Add the sea scallops and cover until poached, about 2 to 3 minutes. Do not overcook. Remove the scallops and drain. Add the bay scallops to the heated wine and cover. Remove after 2 to 3 minutes and drain. Do not overcook. Arrange all of the scallops on the greens.

In a food processor, combine the eggs, egg yolks, lemon juice, vinegar, orange concentrate, and salt, and blend. With the processor running, slowly add the peanut oil. Thin with half-and-half to pouring consistency and drizzle the dressing over the salads.

Serves 4.

TALLGRASS
1006 S. State
Lockport, Illinois 60441
(815) 838-5566

Zesty Spring Chicken Salad

2 cups dry white wine
2 chicken breasts (8 ounces each),
   skinned and boned
Juice of 1 orange
½ cup sour cream
½ cup mayonnaise
3 ounces bleu cheese (or to taste)
Salt

White pepper
8 ounces fresh spinach, rinsed in
   several changes of cold
   water, dried, and stemmed
1 seedless orange, peeled
   and segmented
4 ounces pistachio nuts, shelled

To prepare the chicken:
Bring the white wine to a bare simmer in a medium-sized skillet. Place the chicken breasts in the wine and poach until they turn white and are firm to the touch. Remove and chill the breasts.

To prepare the dressing:
Combine the orange juice, sour cream, and mayonnaise. Mix until smooth. Add the bleu cheese and mix. Add salt and pepper to taste. Mix thoroughly and refrigerate.

To assemble the salad:
Divide the spinach among four salad plates. Cut the chicken breasts in half lengthwise, leaving four equal portions. Cut these portions widthwise into 7 slices each. Place each portion on the spinach and fan out the meat. Drizzle the bleu cheese dressing on top of each salad. Garnish with orange segments and pistachios.

Serves 4.

ASH MANOR
1600 W. Diversey Parkway
Chicago, Illinois 60614
(312) 248-1600

Thai Beef Salad

1½ tablespoons vegetable oil
½ pound flank steak, sliced
      very thinly and cut into
      pieces 2 inches long
½ cup thinly sliced onion
4 tablespoons freshly squeezed
      lime juice
4 tablespoons nampla
      (fish sauce)*
½ teaspoon sugar
½ teaspoon ground red chili
1 to 2 cucumbers, quartered
      lengthwise and
      thinly sliced
1 tablespoon chopped cilantro,
      for garnish
1 tablespoon chopped scallions,
      for garnish

Heat the oil in a frying pan or wok. Add the beef and stir-fry until it is medium-rare to medium. (Or grill the flank steak on a barbeque and then slice thinly.) Put the beef into a bowl and add the onion, lime juice, fish sauce, sugar, and red chili. Mix well.

Place the cucumber slices on a platter. Arrange the beef salad on top of the cucumbers. Garnish with the cilantro and scallions. May be served chilled, if desired.

Serves 2 to 4.

*Available at Oriental grocery stores.

SIAM CAFÉ
4712 N. Sheridan
Chicago, Illinois 60640
(312) 769-6602

Insalata di Bistecca (Italian Steak Salad)

2 pounds eye of round
1 small red onion, sliced julienne
1 large tomato, peeled, seeded,
    and diced
3 ounces arugula, washed,
    dried, and torn into
    bite-sized pieces
1/4 cup extra virgin olive oil
2 tablespoons dried oregano
Salt
Freshly ground black pepper
Italian black olives, for garnish
Imported Parmesan cheese,
    for garnish

Trim the meat of any excess fat. Grill the beef until medium-rare, then chill. Slice the beef into julienne strips. In a large bowl, mix the beef and onion with the tomato and arugula. Toss with the olive oil and oregano, and add salt and pepper to taste. Arrange the insalata on salad plates. If desired, garnish with Italian black olives and a small slice of imported Parmesan cheese. Serve chilled or at room temperature.

Serves 6 to 8.

CAFÉ SPIAGGIA
980 N. Michigan Avenue
Chicago, Illinois 60611
(312) 280-2764

Steak Salad

For the salad:
6 ounces beef tenderloin (end cut)
    or sirloin
Salt
Pepper
4 iceberg lettuce leaves
Small bunch watercress
8 leaves Belgian endive
4 thin slices avocado
    or cantaloupe
Black olives, for garnish

1 teaspoon Dijon mustard
1 teaspoon sugar
Juice of 1 lemon
1½ ounces Rhine wine
1½ ounces spinach, pre-cooked,
    chopped into small pieces
2 egg yolks
Salt
Pepper
Black olives, for garnish

For the dressing:
1 cup mayonnaise
1 cup tartar sauce

Grill or sauté the meat medium-rare to medium, adding salt and pepper to taste. Cool the meat for 1 to 2 minutes. Cut into 1-inch cubes.

Arrange the lettuce, watercress, and endive along with a thin slice of avocado or cantaloupe on a serving dish. Place the meat on top of the salad.

Mix all of the dressing ingredients thoroughly. Pour over the steak salad when ready to serve. Add black olives for garnish.

Serves 4.

THE BERGHOFF
17 W. Adams
Chicago, Illinois 60603
(312) 427-3170

Famoso Pasta Salad

¼ cup extra virgin olive oil
4 cloves garlic, peeled
    and minced
¾ pound red onion, peeled and
    cut into half circles
1½ pounds red bell peppers,
    cored and seeded,
    cut lengthwise into
    ½-inch strips
¼ cup red wine vinegar
3 pounds tomatoes, peeled,
    seeded, and chopped,
    keeping juice
1 pound rigatoni
1½ cups Italian black olives,
    pitted and sliced

Heat the olive oil in a saucepan. Add the garlic and the onion and sauté.
Add the peppers after the onion softens. Sauté for 6 to 7 more minutes.
Add the vinegar and cook, covered, for 3 more minutes.

Add the tomatoes. Cook uncovered until the tomatoes give off their juice
and the juices thicken. Let cool. While the tomatoes are cooking, cook
the rigatoni in a large pot of boiling, salted water until al dente.

Combine the pasta with the sauce and the black olives. Serve at room
temperature.

Serves 6 to 8.

CONVITO ITALIANO
11 E. Chestnut Street
Chicago, Illinois 60611
(312) 943-2984

Hiyashi-Chuka-Soba   (Cold Noodle Salad)

4 tablespoons rice vinegar
2 tablespoons soy sauce
1½ tablespoons sugar
4 tablespoons fish or chicken
   stock
1 to 2 drops sesame oil
4 packages Ramen noodles
2 eggs
½ teaspoon salad oil

4 slices cooked chicken or ham,
   cut into strips
1 small cucumber, cut into strips
1 medium avocado, cut into
   thick strips
1 medium tomato, sliced and
   each slice halved
¼ head of lettuce, shredded
   into strips

Mix together the vinegar, soy sauce, sugar, fish or chicken stock, and sesame oil. Set aside.

Cook the noodles according to package directions. Rinse them under cold water in a colander. Beat the eggs and cook as a thin omelette in ½ teaspoon salad oil. Cut the finished omelette into strips.

Place the noodles on a plate. Arrange the chicken or ham, cucumber, avocado, tomato, lettuce, and egg strips in pie-shaped wedges on top, covering the noodles. Pour the sauce over the salad before serving.

Serves 4.

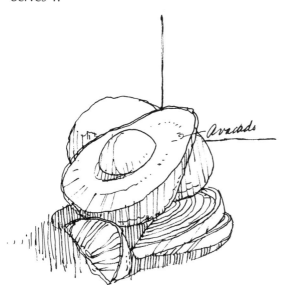

avocado

NEW JAPAN
1322 Chicago Avenue
Evanston, Illinois 60201
(312) 475-5980

Yum Ma Kua   (Eggplant Salad)

2 or 3 small, slender
    purple eggplants
Chili paste*
1 tablespoon corn oil
½ teaspoon minced garlic
    (or more to taste)
1 tablespoon fish sauce*
12 to 15 fresh mint leaves
1 or 2 hard boiled eggs,
    thinly sliced

Grill or broil the eggplants whole for about 15 minutes, turning 2 or 3 times. Let the eggplants cool. Peel each eggplant and cut into 1-inch long sections. Add chili paste to taste. Mix carefully and set aside.

Heat the corn oil in a wok over medium heat. Add the garlic and sauté until golden. Add the fish sauce, stirring constantly. Add the seasoned eggplant and 10 of the mint leaves while stir-frying. Remove from the wok to a serving plate and garnish with the remaining mint leaves and egg slices.

Serves 3 to 4.

*Available at Oriental grocery stores.

ANANDA
941 N. State Street
Chicago, Illinois 60610
(312) 944-7440

Patatas con Alioli (Garlic Potato Salad)

*15 tiny red potatoes (about
        3 pounds)
1 cup mayonnaise
4 cloves garlic, minced
4 tablespoons minced
        fresh parsley
½ teaspoon salt
Freshly ground white pepper*

Boil the potatoes in water to cover until they are tender but not mushy, about 10 to 20 minutes. Drain the potatoes and allow to cool. Peel and cut them in half. Mix the remaining ingredients in a large bowl. Add the potatoes. Toss gently. Let stand one hour before serving.

Serves 4.

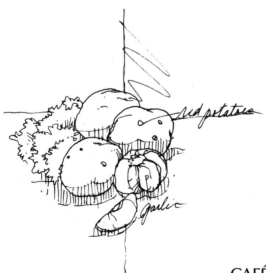

CAFÉ BA-BA-REEBA!
2024 N. Halsted
Chicago, Illinois 60614
(312) 935-5000

Caesar Salad

¼ cup Worcestershire sauce
1½ cups mayonnaise
1 ounce anchovy paste
⅛ cup lemon juice,
    freshly squeezed
1 teaspoon black pepper,
    freshly ground
6 slices best-quality white bread,
    crust removed
2 cloves garlic, cut in half
    lengthwise
2 bunches romaine
4 teaspoons imported Parmesan
    cheese, freshly grated
1 tomato, cut into 6 wedges
6 anchovies

Make a dressing by blending the Worcestershire sauce, mayonnaise, anchovy paste, lemon juice, and black pepper in a food processor until creamy. Set aside.

Toast the bread in an oven until golden brown. Rub both sides of the toasted bread with the cut side of a clove of garlic. Cut the bread into small cubes.

Tear the romaine into bite-sized pieces. Rinse and drain. Combine with the Parmesan cheese and the dressing. Toss gently. Serve on chilled plates. Garnish each salad with a tomato wedge, an anchovy, and garlic croutons.

Serves 6.

SHAW'S CRAB HOUSE
21 E. Hubbard Street
Chicago, Illinois 60611
(312) 527-2722

Garbage Salad

Romaine lettuce, iceberg lettuce,
    and fresh spinach—enough
    for 6 salads
1 can (14 ounces) artichoke
    hearts, drained, rinsed,
    and quartered
1 can (14 ounces) hearts of palm,
    drained, rinsed, and sliced
1 cup peeled and diced jicama
1 cup peeled and diced turnips
1 cup diced cactus leaves*
1 cup peeled and diced carrots
2 medium tomatoes, seeded and
    diced
½ cup diced red cabbage
8 ounces bacon, cooked and
    crumbled

Clean the romaine and iceberg lettuce and the spinach. Tear into bite-sized pieces and fill 6 bowls with a mixture of the three greens. Chill the filled bowls in the refrigerator.

Toss together the remaining ingredients. Arrange on top of the salad in the bowls. Serve with your favorite dressing.

Serves 6.

*Available at specialty markets.

SUPERIOR STREET CAFÉ
311 W. Superior Street
Chicago, Illinois 60610
(312) 787-4160

Nick's Classic Salad

3 ounces fresh spinach,
   washed, stemmed, and
   finely chopped
1 ounce leeks, white part
   only, washed and
   finely chopped
2 cups mayonnaise
1 teaspoon freshly squeezed
   lemon juice

¾ teaspoon Maggie Seasoning
2 anchovy fillets
White pepper
An assortment of your favorite
   salad greens, torn into
   bite-sized pieces (enough
   for 4 salads)
Bay shrimp, for garnish

Combine the spinach, leeks, mayonnaise, lemon juice, Maggie
Seasoning, anchovies, and a pinch of white pepper. Mix well and chill
for several hours. Toss the dressing with the salad greens and divide
among 4 salad plates. Garnish each salad with bay shrimp.

Serves 4.

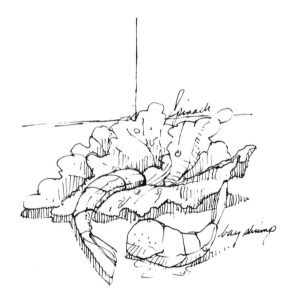

NICK'S FISHMARKET
One First National Plaza
Chicago, Illinois 60603
(312) 621-0200

Celery Seed Dressing

1 cup sugar
1 teaspoon dry mustard
2 tablespoons celery seed
1 cup white vinegar
3 tablespoons grated onion
2 cups salad oil

Mix together the sugar, dry mustard, and celery seed. Pour the vinegar into a glass bowl. Whisk the dry ingredients and grated onion thoroughly into the vinegar. Slowly whisk in the salad oil, and continue whisking for 3 to 5 minutes.

Refrigerate in a glass container. Shake vigorously before serving over your favorite mixed greens.

Yields 1 quart.

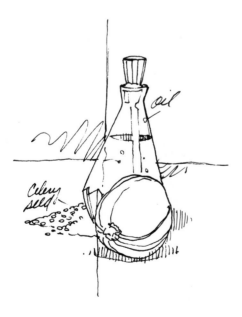

ANN SATHER
929 W. Belmont Avenue
Chicago, Illinois 60657
(312) 348-2378

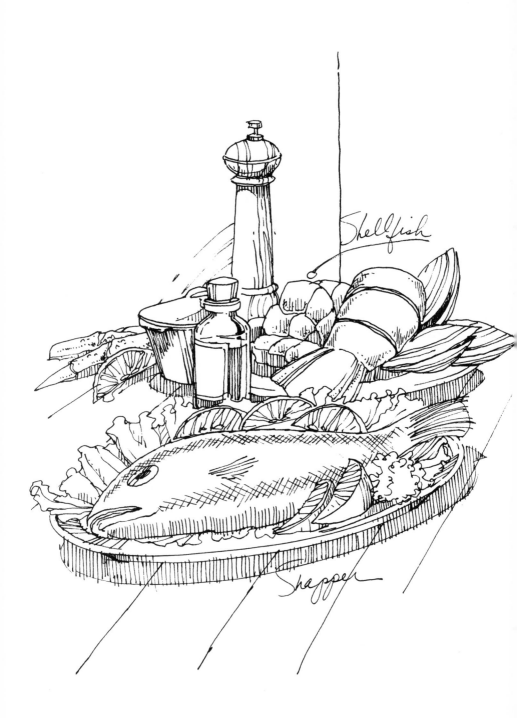

Shellfish

Snapper

Seafood

Grilled Bluefish with Citrus Vinaigrette and Herbs

Juice of 4 oranges
Juice of 2 lemons
Juice of 2 limes
Extra virgin olive oil
Salt
Freshly ground black pepper
4 medium-sized bluefish fillets,
    boned and skinned
1 orange, peeled and sectioned,
    for garnish
Chopped fresh herbs (parsley,
    marjoram, and rosemary,
    for example), for garnish

To prepare the vinaigrette:
Mix the orange, lemon, and lime juices. Add double the amount of oil as you have citrus juices. Season with salt and pepper to taste.

To prepare the fish:
Preheat the broiler or grill. Brush the bluefish fillets with olive oil to prevent them from sticking to the hot grill. Season the fillets with salt and pepper. Grill the bluefish until just done. Do not overcook. Remove immediately to a serving platter. Pour some citrus vinaigrette on the fish and garnish with orange sections and chopped fresh herbs.

Serves 4.

FOLEY'S ON OHIO
211 E. Ohio
Chicago, Illinois 60601
(312) 645-1261

Catfish Vietnamese Style

2 tablespoons plus 1 teaspoon
    sugar, divided
4 tablespoons water, divided
½ cup sliced onion
¼ teaspoon salt
4 catfish steaks, about 1 pound
    total

1 cup chicken broth, preferably
    homemade
4 scallion stems, cut in 2-inch
    pieces
1 tablespoon vegetable oil
Freshly ground black pepper
1½ cups cooked rice

To make the dark sugar syrup, put 2 tablespoons of sugar and 2 tablespoons of water into a small, heavy saucepan or skillet. Cook over high heat for about 4 minutes, until the mixture starts to turn golden. Stir the mixture constantly until it darkens and steam rises. Remove from the heat immediately, continuing to stir. Carefully pour in 1 tablespoon of water, stirring constantly. Be very careful because the mixture will spatter. Stir in the remaining tablespoon of water. Continuing to stir, return to high heat for 2 minutes. Pour the syrup into a small cup and set aside to cool.

Place the onion in a heavy aluminum or enameled cast-iron 1-quart pot. Sprinkle with 1 teaspoon sugar, the salt, and ½ tablespoon syrup. Rub 1 tablespoon of syrup onto each side of the fish steaks. Lay the fish steaks over the onion. Pour the chicken broth over the catfish. Drizzle the remaining syrup over the broth.

Cover the pan partially and place over very high heat. When the liquid boils, remove the lid. Continue to boil the mixture over the highest heat until slightly thickened, about 10 minutes. Lay the scallion stems over the fish. Pour the vegetable oil over the fish and season with black pepper to taste. Continue to cook for about 5 minutes until the broth thickens to a sauce-like consistency. Remove from the heat and serve with cooked rice.

Serves 2.

PASTEUR
4759 N. Sheridan Road
Chicago, Illinois 60640
(312) 271-6673

Salmon with American Caviar, Basil, and Shallots

4 fillets of salmon, 6 to 8 ounces
    each, skinned
Salt
Pepper
10 tablespoons (1¼ sticks)
    unsalted butter
4 medium-sized red potatoes,
    scrubbed, unpeeled,
    and diced

3 large shallots, peeled and sliced
1½ cups snow peas, blanched
    and julienned
20 fresh basil leaves, chopped
1 cup sliced fresh mushrooms
¼ cup water
¼ cup dry white wine
2 ounces salmon caviar

Season the salmon with salt and pepper to taste on each side. Preheat two nonstick sauté pans over medium heat. Melt half of the butter slowly in each pan.

When the butter is melted, sauté the potatoes and shallots in one pan. Add the salmon fillets to the other pan, the side with the grey fat facing up. Sauté for about 3 minutes. Turn the salmon with a spatula and cook for a few more minutes. Do not let the salmon overcook. Gently remove the salmon from the pan. Add the snow peas, basil, mushrooms, water, and wine to the potatoes and shallots. Heat to a simmer and season with salt and pepper to taste.

Place each salmon fillet in the center of a plate and surround with the sauce. Top with caviar.

Serves 4.

GORDON
500 N. Clark Street
Chicago, Illinois 60610
(312) 467-9780

Alaskan Salmon Artico

2 pounds salmon fillets, skinned
4 tablespoons unsalted butter
6 green onions, white and green
    parts, chopped
4 tablespoons flour, divided
¾ cup fish stock or bottled clam
    juice
1 cup half-and-half
Salt
Pepper
¼ cup olive oil
½ pound fresh spinach fettucine
1 ounce red lumpfish caviar
1 ounce black lumpfish caviar

Cut the salmon into strips 3 inches long and ½ inch wide. Set aside.

Melt the butter in a skillet over medium-high heat and sauté the green onions for about a minute. Add 2 tablespoons of flour and cook, stirring constantly for 2 minutes. Add the fish stock or bottled clam juice and the half-and-half. Simmer until the sauce is thick enough to coat the back of a spoon. Add salt and pepper to taste.

Heat the olive oil in a skillet over medium heat until hot but not smoking. Roll the salmon strips in the remaining flour. Sauté the salmon on both sides until lightly browned.

Cook the fettucine in a large pot of boiling water until *al dente*. Drain well. Divide the pasta among four warm serving plates. Arrange the salmon strips on top of the pasta. Pour the sauce over the salmon and pasta, and sprinkle red and black caviar over all.

Serves 4.

LA STRADA
155 N. Michigan Avenue
Chicago, Illinois 60601
(312) 565-2200

Grilled Sockeye Salmon with Citrus Relish

3 oranges
4 pink grapefruit
2 teaspoons minced cilantro
White pepper
1 tablespoon honey
1 tablespoon sugar
4 tablespoons water

1 tablespoon freshly squeezed
   lemon juice
3 pounds fresh North Pacific
   sockeye salmon fillets, cut
   into 8-ounce portions
Lemon slices for garnish

To prepare the citrus relish:
Peel the oranges and the grapefruit and separate them into sections. Place the sections in a bowl and reserve any juice. Add the cilantro to the fruit. Season with pepper to taste.

In a small saucepan, combine the honey, sugar, water, and reserved citrus juice over low heat. Cook until the honey and sugar are dissolved, stirring constantly. Cool. Add the lemon juice. Pour this mixture over the sectioned fruit.

To prepare the fish:
Place the salmon fillets on a hot charcoal grill, skin side down, and grill for about 3 minutes. (The skin should be charred.) Turn the fillets and cook on the other side for 3 minutes. Fillets should be medium rare. Place the fillets on individual, warm serving plates and garnish with the citrus relish and the lemon slices.

Serves 6.

SHAW'S CRAB HOUSE
21 E. Hubbard Street
Chicago, Illinois 60611
(312) 527-2722

Salmon in Dill Beurre Blanc

2 cups dry white wine
4 tablespoons chopped shallots
2 tablespoons chopped fresh dill
1 cup heavy cream
½ teaspoon Tabasco sauce
1 cup chicken stock,
        preferably homemade
3 sticks salted butter, softened
        to room temperature
4 salmon fillets, 8 ounces each
1 tablespoon oil
Salt
Freshly ground black pepper
Dill sprigs, for garnish
Lemon wedges, for garnish

In a saucepan, combine the white wine, shallots, dill, cream, Tabasco sauce, and chicken stock. Bring to a boil and reduce the mixture to about 1 cup. Over low heat, add the butter, 1 tablespoon at a time, stirring constantly with a wire whisk. Place the saucepan in a water bath to keep the sauce warm (about 110°) while the fish fillets are grilling.

Coat the salmon fillets with oil and season with salt and pepper to taste. Grill the fillets until firm and tender. Do not overcook. Transfer the fillets to warm serving plates. Nap each fillet with ¼ cup of the sauce. Garnish with a sprig of dill and a lemon wedge.

Serves 4.

THE CHESTNUT STREET GRILL
Water Tower Place
845 N. Michigan Avenue
Chicago, Illinois 60611
(312) 280-2720

Salmon with Mustard, Peppercorns, and Avocado Salsa

For the avocado salsa:
1 cucumber, peeled, seeded,
  and diced
2 tomatoes, peeled, seeded,
  and diced
1 small red onion, diced
1 small yellow or red bell pepper,
  cored, seeded, and diced
1 cup freshly squeezed lime juice,
  or to taste
4 teaspoons chopped cilantro

1 tablespoon olive oil
Salt
1 avocado

For the salmon:
4 salmon fillets (6 ounces each),
  skin and bones removed
Coarse-grained mustard
3/4 teaspoon coarsely crushed
  black peppercorns
1/4 cup clarified butter

To prepare the avocado salsa:
Combine the cucumber, tomato, red onion, and bell pepper. Add the lime juice, cilantro, olive oil, and salt to taste. Mix well. Refrigerate the mixture for 2 hours or more to blend flavors. Before serving, cut the avocado flesh into 1/4-inch pieces and mix with the other ingredients.

To prepare the salmon:
Rub the salmon fillets with a thin coat of mustard on all sides. Sprinkle black peppercorns on both sides of the fillets. Heat a sauté pan over medium-high heat. Add the clarified butter. Add the salmon fillets and sauté for 2 to 3 minutes. Turn the fish and cook for about 2 minutes more, depending on the size of the fillets. Place the salsa on 4 serving plates and top with the salmon fillets.

Serves 4.

THE 95th
John Hancock Center
875 N. Michigan Avenue
Chicago, Illinois 60611
(312) 787-9596

Senagrida Skaras (Broiled Red Snapper)

1 whole red snapper
   (1 to 2 pounds)
1 teaspoon salt per pound of fish
¼ cup olive oil
¼ cup freshly squeezed
   lemon juice

1 teaspoon oregano
Lemon slices, for garnish
Tomato wedges, for garnish
Cucumber slices, for garnish

Preheat the broiler.

Scale and clean the fish thoroughly in cold water, or have this done at your fish market. Pat the fish dry. Make a ¼-inch deep slit nearly the entire length of each side of the fish. Place the fish on a broiler pan.

In a glass bowl, whisk together the salt, oil, lemon juice, and oregano. Brush the top side of the fish with this mixture. Broil the fish approximately 10 inches from the flame for about 10 minutes. Turn the fish over carefully. Brush the other side of the fish with the oil and lemon juice mixture. Broil 6 more minutes or until the fish is cooked through. Remove the fish to a platter. Pour the rest of the oil and lemon juice mixture over the fish. Garnish with lemon slices, tomato wedges, and cucumber slices.

Serves 2.

COURTYARDS OF PLAKA
340 S. Halsted
Chicago, Illinois 60606
(312) 263-0767

Snapper Veracruzana

6 portions (8 ounces each)
 Florida red snapper,
 cleaned and filleted
½ tablespoon salt
White pepper to taste
5 tablespoons olive oil
2 limes, quartered
1 medium onion, thinly sliced
2 large cloves garlic, thinly sliced
¼ cup extra virgin olive oil
2 pounds tomatoes,
 peeled, seeded, and
 coarsely chopped

1 bay leaf
¼ teaspoon oregano
12 green olives, pitted and halved
2 tablespoons capers, drained
 and rinsed
2 chiles en escabeche or 1½ fresh
 jalapeño peppers*
¼ cup dry white wine
Fresh cilantro leaves

Preheat the oven to 425°.

Place the fish in a large baking dish. Season with salt and white pepper. Drizzle the 5 tablespoons of olive oil over the fish and squeeze ½ lime over all. Set aside.

Sauté the onion and garlic in the olive oil until soft but not browned. Add the tomatoes and the remaining ingredients up to and including the *chiles*. Turn up the heat and cook until some of the juices have evaporated, about 5 to 10 minutes. Swirl in the white wine, cook one minute more, and remove from the heat. Taste and correct the seasoning. Pour this mixture onto the fish fillets. Bake them until done—about 8 to 10 minutes or longer, depending on the thickness of the fillets. Place the fillets on individual serving plates. Garnish each plate with a lime quarter and whole cilantro leaves.

Serves 6.

Chiles en escabeche are available at Mexican grocery stores.

BODEGA BAY CAFÉ
Sherman at Grove
Evanston, Illinois 60201
(312) 328-8540

Paupiettes of Sole Lady Ash

For the fish:
21 to 25 (½ pound) shrimp,
    peeled and deveined
    (reserve 8 with tails intact)
1 egg
⅓ cup heavy cream
Cayenne pepper
Nutmeg
Salt
Freshly ground black pepper
1 tablespoon freshly
    chopped parsley
4 sole fillets, about 6 ounces each

For the sauce:
1 cup dry white wine
4 large shallots, minced
2 tablespoons chopped fresh basil
⅛ cup heavy cream (optional)
8 tablespoons (1 stick)
    unsalted butter, cut
    into tablespoon pieces

To prepare the fish:
In a food processor, purée the shrimp. Add the egg, ⅓ cup of cream, and a pinch each of cayenne and nutmeg. Add salt and pepper to taste. Add the parsley and process until well blended. Refrigerate, covered, for 30 minutes. Steam the remaining 8 shrimp. Preheat the oven to 325°. Lay the fillets out flat. Spread the shrimp mixture over each fillet, leaving a ½-inch border on all sides. Roll up the fillets, starting with the tail end. Place the fillets with the fold down on a baking sheet. Bake for 8 to 10 minutes.

To prepare the sauce:
In a medium saucepan, simmer the wine, shallots, basil, and cream, if desired, until the mixture is reduced by half. Remove the sauce from the heat and gradually whisk in pieces of butter until the sauce is smooth and creamy. To serve, place a small pool of the sauce in the center of each plate. Place one paupiette in the middle of the plate. Put one shrimp at each end of the sole with the tails facing clockwise. Nap the paupiettes lightly with the sauce. Serve immediately.

Serves 4.

ASH MANOR
1600 W. Diversey Parkway
Chicago, Illinois 60614
(312) 248-1600

Sole en Sacque

4 tablespoons unsalted butter
1 small onion, finely chopped
4 tablespoons flour
½ teaspoon McCormick's
    seafood seasoning
¼ teaspoon salt
¼ teaspoon black pepper
Nutmeg
2 cups half-and-half
¼ cup sherry
½ pound cooked shrimp,
    coarsely chopped

¼ cup pitted black olives,
    sliced or chopped
¼ cup fresh mushrooms,
    chopped
6 small paper bags
Corn oil
12 fillets of grey sole,
    3 to 4 ounces each
6 thin slices of smoked ham or
    Canadian bacon
Paprika

To prepare the sauce:
In a saucepan, melt the butter over low heat. Add the onion and sauté until translucent. Add the flour and cook for 2 minutes, stirring constantly with a wooden spoon. Add the seafood seasoning, salt, pepper, and nutmeg. Add the half-and-half and the sherry and cook over low heat for about 5 minutes until the mixture thickens. Add the shrimp, olives, and mushrooms and sauté briefly.

To prepare the sole:
Preheat the oven to 450°. Brush the outsides of the six paper lunch bags with corn oil and lay them on their sides on an oiled baking sheet. Lay a slice of ham on a spatula. Place a sole fillet on top of the ham. Spoon a layer of the sauce on the fillet and lay another fillet on top of it. Spoon a bit of sauce over the second fillet. Sprinkle with paprika and insert into a paper bag. Repeat this procedure until all the fillets are used. Seal each bag by folding over the top several times. Bake for 15 minutes. Serve the sole on individual plates.

Serves 6.

THE WATERFRONT
16 W. Maple
Chicago, Illinois 60610
(312) 943-7494

Whitefish and Shrimp in Walnut Cream Sauce

¼ cup apple cider vinegar
2 tablespoons chopped shallots
1 cup fish stock or bottled
    clam juice
¼ cup dry vermouth
⅛ teaspoon white pepper
1 cup whipping cream
½ pound (2 sticks) unsalted butter
¼ cup walnut oil
Salt
4 fillets of Lake Superior whitefish,
    bones removed

8 large fresh shrimp, peeled
    and deveined
8 tablespoons (1 stick) clarified,
    unsalted butter
Walnuts, for garnish
Zucchini, yellow squash, and
    carrots, cut into julienne
    matchsticks and blanched,
    for garnish

Place the vinegar, shallots, fish stock or clam juice, vermouth, and white pepper in a heavy saucepan. Reduce over high heat to 1 tablespoon of liquid.

Add the whipping cream and bring to a boil. Add the ½ pound of butter, stirring constantly. Add the walnut oil, stirring constantly. Add salt to taste. Transfer the saucepan to a water bath to keep warm.

Sauté the whitefish and shrimp in the clarified butter until just done. Do not overcook. Arrange the fillets and shrimp on 4 warm plates and pour the sauce around the fish. Garnish with the walnuts and vegetables.

Serves 4.

TALLGRASS
1006 S. State
Lockport, Illinois 60441
(815) 838-5566

Calamari Steak Ricci

8 tablespoons unsalted butter
1 cup asparagus tips
1 cup sliced fresh mushrooms
¼ pound small shrimp,
    peeled and deveined
4 tablespoons freshly squeezed
    lemon juice

Salt
Freshly ground black pepper
4 calamari steaks, 5 ounces each
Flour for dredging
2 eggs, lightly beaten
4 tablespoons olive oil
1 tablespoon chopped fresh dill

To prepare the Ricci sauce:
Melt the butter in a sauté pan. Sauté the asparagus tips and mushrooms over medium heat. When the vegetables are crisp-tender, add the shrimp and the lemon juice and cook until the shrimp turn pink. Salt and pepper to taste.

To prepare the steaks:
Lightly flour the calamari steaks and dip them into the beaten eggs. Sauté in hot oil about 2 minutes per side until the steaks are golden brown and tender. Place the steaks on warm plates, and cover with the Ricci sauce. Garnish with fresh dill and serve.

Serves 4.

NICK'S FISHMARKET
One First National Plaza
Chicago, Illinois 60603
(312) 621-0200

New Orleans Crabcakes

¼ teaspoon salt
1½ tablespoons paprika
1½ tablespoons freshly ground
  black pepper
1 teaspoon onion powder,
  or less to taste
½ teaspoon cayenne pepper
¼ teaspoon thyme
¼ teaspoon oregano
¼ teaspoon white pepper
1½ tablespoons minced garlic
⅓ to ½ cup breadcrumbs
1½ tablespoons Romano cheese
1 tablespoon minced parsley

1 pound fresh or frozen crabmeat,
  picked over
½ cup mayonnaise
2 tablespoons chopped scallions,
  white part only
3 tablespoons chopped green
  bell pepper
4 tablespoons diced onion
2 tablespoons chopped celery
Tabasco sauce to taste
1 tablespoon Worcestershire
  sauce
Corn oil

Mix the salt, paprika, black pepper, onion powder, cayenne, thyme, oregano, and white pepper. Then add the minced garlic. Reserve this seasoning mixture.

Mix the breadcrumbs, Romano cheese, and parsley. Reserve.

In a bowl, blend 1½ teaspoons of the seasoning mix with all of the remaining ingredients except the corn oil. Form into 1½-inch balls. Roll them in the seasoned breadcrumbs and flatten into ½-inch thick patties.

Heat 2 tablespoons of corn oil in a skillet over medium heat. Sauté the crabcakes in batches until golden brown. Replenish the corn oil as needed. Serve warm.

Serves 6 to 8.

DIXIE BAR & GRILL
225 W. Chicago Avenue
Chicago, Illinois 60610
(312) 642-3336

Lobster in Vanilla Sauce

For the court bouillon and lobster:
1 carrot, roughly chopped
1 large onion, coarsely chopped
1 rib celery, coarsely chopped
A few parsley stems
1 clove garlic, peeled
4 to 5 black peppercorns
2 bay leaves
Pinch of thyme
Pinch of tarragon
Salt
2 quarts fish stock or water
1 vanilla bean, sliced in half
2 quarts dry white wine
2 to 3 branches seaweed
     (optional)

2 lobsters, about 1½ pounds
     each, preferably live

For the vanilla sauce:
3 to 4 shallots, chopped
1 teaspoon unsalted butter
2 ounces dry white wine
1 vanilla bean
1 quart whipping cream
1 ounce fish glacé (or 1 ounce
     of lobster tomalley)
1 pound bay scallops
Salt
Freshly ground black pepper

To prepare the court bouillon:
Simmer all the ingredients up to and including the fish stock or water for
1 hour. Add the vanilla bean and white wine and bring to a boil. Add the
optional seaweed and the lobsters and boil 8 to 10 minutes. Remove the
lobsters. When the lobsters have cooled, remove the meat from the tails
and the claws, slice the tail meat into medallions, and reserve.

To prepare the vanilla sauce:
Briefly sauté the shallots in the butter. Add the white wine and the
vanilla bean. Reduce until almost dry. Add the cream and the fish glacé
or lobster tomalley. Bring to a boil. Reduce heat and simmer for about
5 minutes. At the last minute, add the scallops just to warm. Add salt and
pepper to taste. Arrange the lobster meat on individual serving plates
and top with the sauce.

Serves 4.

FROGGY'S
306 Greenbay Road
Highwood, Illinois 60040
(312) 433-7080

Shrimp Caribe

1½ pounds rotini
1 pint whipping cream
1 teaspoon caribe spice (crushed
          dried chiles), or to taste
1 tablespoon Italian seasoning mix
½ tablespoon garlic powder
Salt
½ tablespoon butter
24 shrimp, peeled and deveined
1 green bell pepper, cored,
          seeded, and thinly sliced
1 yellow bell pepper, cored,
          seeded, and thinly sliced
1 red bell pepper, cored, seeded,
          and thinly sliced

Cook the rotini in a large pot of boiling, salted water until *al dente*.
Drain well.

In a saucepan, heat the whipping cream, caribe spice, Italian seasoning,
and garlic powder. Add salt to taste. Bring to a boil and then set aside.

In a large skillet, melt the butter over medium-high heat. Sauté the shrimp
and peppers until the shrimp turn white. Add the caribe sauce and rotini.
Mix together. Remove from heat and divide among 4 warm pasta bowls.

Serves 4.

BLUE MESA
1729 N. Halsted
Chicago, Illinois 60614
(312) 944-5990

Shrimp Chippewa

1½ cups (3 sticks) unsalted butter,
    cut into 1-tablespoon pieces
4 cloves garlic, minced
1 cup scallions, thinly sliced
48 medium shrimp, peeled,
    cleaned, and deveined
¾ pound fresh mushrooms,
    cleaned and sliced

6 cups strong chicken stock,
    preferably homemade
¼ cup finely chopped parsley
1 teaspoon cayenne pepper
Salt

Melt ½ cup butter (1 stick) in a very large skillet. Sauté the garlic and
scallions for 1 minute. Add the shrimp and the mushrooms. Sauté until
the shrimp begin to turn pink and the mushrooms begin to wilt, about
2 to 3 minutes.

Add the chicken stock and parsley. Bring to a boil. Add the cayenne
pepper and remove from heat. While stirring constantly, add the
remaining butter, 1 piece at a time after each slice has melted.
A slightly thickened sauce will form.

Serve in warm soup plates with French bread for dipping.

Serves 6.

THE WINNETKA GRILL
64 Green Bay Road
Winnetka, Illinois 60093
(312) 441-6444

Shrimp à la Grecque

2 tablespoons olive oil
1/4 cup finely diced onion
1 clove garlic, minced
1 pound plum tomatoes, peeled,
    seeded, and chopped
1 tablespoon tomato paste
1 bay leaf
Tarragon
Basil
Thyme
Sugar

Cayenne pepper
20 large shrimp in shells, rinsed
    thoroughly in cold water
Salt
White pepper
2 tablespoons vegetable oil
5 tablespoons unsalted butter
1 or 2 whole garlic cloves, peeled
6 ounces feta cheese, cut into
    1/2-inch cubes
1 ounce Pernod or brandy

Heat the olive oil in a large skillet. Sauté the onion and minced garlic until the onion is translucent. Add the chopped tomatoes, tomato paste, and bay leaf. Add the tarragon, basil, thyme, sugar, and cayenne pepper to taste. Let this mixture simmer for 30 to 45 minutes. Taste and correct seasoning.

Season the raw shrimp with a dash of salt and a dash of white pepper. Heat the vegetable oil in a large skillet until very hot but not smoking. Sear the shrimp in their shells for approximately 30 seconds. Remove the shrimp and let cool. Peel and clean the shrimp.

In a large skillet, heat the butter and sauté 1 to 2 whole garlic cloves until the butter turns a light brown. Remove the garlic cloves. Add the tomato mixture and the shrimp. Simmer for 2 to 3 minutes. Add the feta cheese. Then pour Pernod or brandy on top of the mixture and light with a match. When the flames subside, serve with white rice.

Serves 4.

JIMMY'S PLACE
3420 N. Elston Avenue
Chicago, Illinois 60618
(312) 539-2999

Shrimp Griglia

20 large shrimp (12 to a pound),
    peeled, deveined, and
    butterflied
4 cups very dry breadcrumbs
4 teaspoons finely minced garlic
4 teaspoons finely minced shallots
4 teaspoons chopped
    fresh parsley
Salt
Freshly ground black pepper
½ pound (2 sticks) salted
    butter, melted

Preheat the oven to 350°.

Slightly pound the butterflied shrimp. Mix the breadcrumbs with the garlic, shallots, and parsley. Add salt and pepper to taste.

Brush the shrimp with the butter and dust them with the seasoned breadcrumbs. Place the shrimp in a large baking dish and bake for about 5 minutes until the shrimp lose their transparency. Do not overcook. Finish the shrimp under the broiler until the breadcrumbs are lightly browned.

Serves 4.

MORTON'S OF CHICAGO
1050 N. State Street
Chicago, Illinois 60610
(312) 266-4820

Szechwan Shrimp with Hot Tomato Sauce

1 pound medium-sized shrimp,
   peeled and deveined
1 egg white, slightly beaten
1 teaspoon dry white wine
1½ tablespoons cornstarch
3 to 4 cups vegetable oil
2 tablespoons chopped onion
1 tablespoon chopped ginger
1 teaspoon chopped celery
2 tablespoons tomato catsup
½ teaspoon salt

3 tablespoons sugar
3 tablespoons chicken broth,
   preferably homemade
2 teaspoons cornstarch, mixed
   with enough water to form
   a thin paste
1 tablespoon hot pepper oil, or
   less to taste
1 teaspoon sesame oil
2 tablespoons chopped green
   onion, for garnish

Marinate the shrimp in the egg white, white wine, and 1½ tablespoons cornstarch. Let stand for 30 minutes.

Heat the vegetable oil in a wok. When the oil is hot but not smoking, add the shrimp. Stir-fry for 2 to 3 minutes or until the shrimp turn white. Do not overcook the shrimp. Remove from the pan and drain on paper towels. Drain the oil from the the pan.

Heat 2 tablespoons of vegetable oil in a wok. Add the chopped onion, ginger, and celery. Stir-fry for 30 to 45 seconds. Add the catsup, salt, sugar, and chicken broth. Boil a few seconds. Add the cornstarch paste to thicken the sauce.

While the sauce thickens, return the shrimp to the pan. Stir. Add the hot pepper oil and sesame oil. Top with the chopped green onions.

Serves 3 to 4.

PINE YARD
924 Church Street
Evanston, Illinois 60201
(312) 475-4940

Camarones à la Veracruzana

(Shrimp Veracruz Style)

4 tablespoons olive oil
1 medium onion, diced
2 cloves garlic, minced
2 large tomatoes, peeled, seeded,
      and chopped
1 tablespoon capers
24 green Spanish olives, pitted
24 fresh jumbo shrimp, peeled,
      deveined, and rinsed
1 cup hot chicken broth,
      preferably homemade
Salt

Heat the oil over medium heat in a large skillet. Sauté the onion and the garlic for a minute or two. Add the tomatoes, capers, olives, and shrimp. Stir once or twice and then pour the hot broth over all. Bring the mixture to a simmer, and simmer for 10 minutes. Add salt to taste. Serve with rice and tortillas.

Serves 4.

LAS MAÑANITAS
3523 N. Halsted
Chicago, Illinois 60657
(312) 528-2109

Cioppino *(Seafood Stew)*

1 large onion, coarsely chopped
1 green bell pepper,
    coarsely chopped
3 large cloves garlic, chopped
⅓ cup olive oil
1 can (16 ounces) tomato sauce
1 can (16 ounces) tomato paste
2 cups red wine
2 bay leaves
⅛ teaspoon thyme
⅛ teaspoon sweet basil
¼ teaspoon paprika
2 teaspoons salt

¼ teaspoon black pepper
Juice of ½ lemon
10 drops Tabasco sauce
Dash of Worcestershire sauce
1 dozen fresh clams
18 large fresh mussels
2 pounds Alaskan king crab legs,
    cut into 3-inch pieces
1½ pounds cod (any firm-fleshed
    fish may be substituted)
1 pound large uncooked shrimp,
    peeled and deveined

In a Dutch oven or large skillet that has a cover, sauté the onion, green pepper, and garlic in the oil for about 5 minutes. Add the tomato sauce, tomato paste, wine, and all the seasonings. Cover and simmer for about an hour. Sauce may be prepared and kept, refrigerated, for several days.

Scrub the clams and mussels and soak them in cold water. Slit the crab legs with shears or a knife. Cut the cod into bite-sized pieces. Pile all the seafood, including the shrimp, in a large pan. Pour on the heated sauce and simmer until the clam and mussel shells open, approximately 20 minutes. Discard any clams and mussels that do not open. Serve in large, shallow soup bowls. Serve with sourdough or French bread.

Serves 6.

Note: This is a very versatile dish. You may substitute any seafood of your choice.

THE WATERFRONT
16 W. Maple
Chicago, Illinois 60610
(312) 943-7494

Seafood Gumbo

For the seasoning mix:
1 teaspoon cayenne pepper or
    red pepper flakes
1 teaspoon paprika
1 teaspoon salt
½ teaspoon white pepper
½ teaspoon black pepper
½ teaspoon dried thyme leaves
½ teaspoon oregano
1 bay leaf, crumbled

For the gumbo:
3 tablespoons shortening or oil
3 tablespoons flour
¾ cup margarine
2 cups diced onion
2 cups diced celery
2 cups diced green pepper
½ cup chopped parsley
1 tablespoon minced garlic

2 cups canned tomatoes, drained
1½ pounds fresh okra, trimmed
    and chopped
5 to 6 cups seafood stock or
    2 cups bottled clam
    juice plus 4 cups water
2 cups fresh or frozen crabmeat,
    picked over
1 dozen oysters, shucked
1½ pounds medium shrimp,
    peeled and deveined
3 tablespoons filé powder
4 cups hot cooked rice

To prepare the seasoning mix:
Combine the seasoning ingredients in a small bowl and set aside.

To prepare the gumbo:
In a heavy pan, make a roux by melting the shortening or heating the oil over low heat. Add the flour and blend thoroughly. Cook for 20 to 30 minutes until the roux is a light brown, stirring constantly with a wooden spoon.

In a heavy soup pot, melt the margarine over medium low heat. Add the onion, celery, green pepper, parsley, garlic, tomatoes, and okra. Turn the heat to high and add the seasoning mix. Cook for 4 to 5 minutes, stirring constantly and scraping the bottom of the pot with the spoon. Reduce the heat and add the roux and the seafood stock. Simmer for 2 hours, stirring occasionally.

Before serving, add the crabmeat, oysters, and shrimp. Cover and turn off the heat. Leave the pot covered just until the seafood is poached, about 10 minutes. Add the filé powder and stir. Do not add the filé powder while the gumbo is boiling or the mixture will become stringy. Place ½ cup of rice in each of 8 bowls and top with the gumbo.

Note: If you wish to make the gumbo in advance, do not add the seafood or filé powder. When you are ready to serve, bring the gumbo to a boil, then lower the heat to simmer and add the seafood. Immediately cover the pot and turn off the heat. Leave covered for 10 minutes. Then add the 3 tablespoons of filé powder. Stir well before serving.

Serves 8.

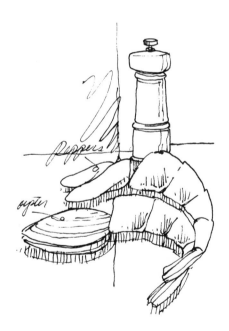

ARMY & LOU'S
420-422 E. 75th Street
Chicago, Illinois 60619
(312) 483-6550

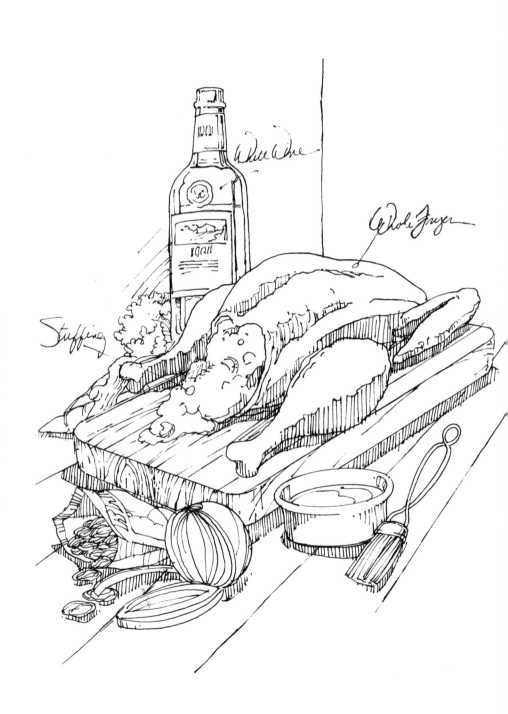

White Wine

Whole Fryer

Stuffing

Poultry

Brandied Chicken with Green Peppercorns

1 tablespoon unsalted butter
4 boneless chicken breasts,
    halved
Salt
2 tablespoons dry vermouth
2 tablespoons minced shallots
4 tablespoons Calvados
    (apple brandy)
1 cup chicken or veal stock
½ cup heavy cream
White pepper
Green peppercorns, cracked
2 tablespoons chopped
    fresh parsley

Preheat the oven to 300°.

Melt the butter in a skillet over medium-high heat. Sauté the chicken, skin side down. Add a pinch of salt. Cook the chicken for about 5 to 10 minutes until brown. Keep the chicken warm in the oven while preparing the sauce.

Heat the vermouth in a sauté pan. Add the shallots and cook until tender. Pour on the brandy and flame. When the flames subside, add the chicken stock or veal stock and the heavy cream. Simmer the mixture until it becomes thick enough to coat the back of a spoon. Season with salt, white pepper, and green peppercorns to taste.

To serve, place some sauce in the middle of a serving plate. Center a chicken breast on top. Sprinkle the parsley over all. Serve with rice.

Serves 4.

CORNELIA'S
750 W. Cornelia
Chicago, Illinois 60657
(312) 248-8333

Chicken alla Cacciatora

1 frying chicken, about 3 to
    3½ pounds, cut into eight
    pieces
Salt
Pepper
Garlic powder
¼ cup olive oil

1 can (16 ounces) imported Italian
    plum tomatoes, crushed
1 pound small, fresh mushrooms,
    whole
12 whole Italian black olives
2 green bell peppers, cored,
    seeded, and diced (optional)

Preheat the oven to 375°. Season the pieces of chicken on both sides with salt, pepper, and garlic powder. In an oven-proof skillet, brown the chicken in the olive oil. Once the chicken is browned, add the tomatoes, mushrooms, whole olives, and optional green peppers. Simmer the ingredients for about 10 minutes. Add a little more salt, pepper, and garlic powder according to taste.

Cover the skillet and bake the chicken in the oven for about 15 minutes. Turn the chicken over and bake for another 15 minutes or until tender. Serve immediately.

Serves 4.

BACCHANALIA
2413 S. Oakley
Chicago, Illinois 60608
(312) 254-6555

Honey Lime Chicken

1¼ cup freshly squeezed
    lime juice
1½ cups honey
1 quart freshly squeezed
    orange juice
½ cup freshly squeezed
    lemon juice
2 frying chickens, 2½ pounds
    each, halved

Preheat the oven to 450°.

Mix ¼ cup of the lime juice and ½ cup of the honey in a small bowl.
Set aside for basting.

Mix the rest of the honey and the juices together to make a marinade.
Marinate the chicken in the refrigerator for at least 4 hours, turning
occasionally.

Drain the chicken and bake for 20 minutes. Then place under the broiler,
basting with the honey-lime mixture, and broil until the chicken is brown
and crispy.

Serves 8.

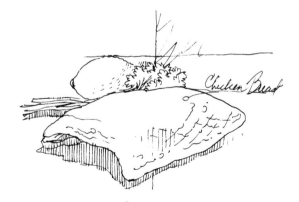

BLUE MESA
1729 N. Halsted
Chicago; Illinois 60614
(312) 944-5990

Lemon Grass Chicken Vietnamese Style

4 chicken drumstick-thigh pieces
2 tablespoons sugar
1 teaspoon salt
2 tablespoons oyster sauce*
2 tablespoons minced
        lemon grass**
2 tablespoons minced garlic
1 teaspoon cayenne pepper
4 tablespoons vegetable oil
3 cups cooked rice

Trim the fat from the chicken. Combine the sugar, salt, oyster sauce, lemon grass, garlic, cayenne pepper, and vegetable oil. Rub this mixture onto the chicken pieces. Set aside to marinate for a minimum of 1 hour or as long as several hours.

Preheat the oven to 450°. Scrape the marinade from the chicken pieces and pat dry. Place the chicken pieces skin side up on a foil-lined baking sheet. Bake in the oven for 25 minutes. Turn the pieces and bake for about 15 minutes longer until the juices at the joints run clear when the chicken is pierced. (The chicken may also be grilled on a barbecue.) Turn the chicken pieces, skin side up, and place under the broiler, if desired, for 2 minutes to brown. Remove from the oven and allow to sit for a few minutes. Serve with rice.

Serves 4.

*Available at Oriental grocery stores.

**Available at Thai and Vietnamese grocery stores. If using fresh lemon grass, mince the lower portion of the stem. If using dried lemon grass, soak for 2 hours in hot water before mincing.

PASTEUR
4759 N. Sheridan Road
Chicago, Illinois 60640
(312) 271-6673

Mole Verde con Pechugas de Pollo   (Green Pumpkinseed Mole with Chicken Breasts)

For the chicken and broth:
½ teaspoon salt
1 small onion, diced
3 large (about 3¾ pounds total)
   chicken breasts, halved

For the sauce:
1 scant cup (about 4 ounces)
   hulled, untoasted
   pumpkinseeds (pepitas)*
12 ounces (about 8 medium)
   tomatillos, husked and
   washed or 1½-cans
   (13 ounces each)
   tomatillos, drained*
Fresh hot green chiles to taste
   (roughly 3 chiles serranos
   or 2 small chiles jalapeños),
   stemmed and seeded*
5 large romaine lettuce leaves
½ medium onion,
   roughly chopped

3 small garlic cloves, peeled
   and roughly chopped
3 large sprigs fresh coriander
   (cilantro) plus more
   for garnish
⅛ teaspoon cumin seeds
   (or a generous ⅛
   teaspoon ground)
6 black peppercorns (or a big
   pinch of ground pepper)
¾-inch cinnamon stick
   (or about ¾ teaspoon
   ground cinnamon)
2 cloves (or a pinch of ground
   cloves)
1½ tablespoons lard or
   vegetable oil
Salt, about ½ teaspoon

Bring 6 cups of water and the salt to a boil in a large saucepan with the diced onion. Add the chicken breasts, skim off any grayish foam that rises during the first minute of simmering. Partially cover and simmer over medium heat for about 12 minutes until the breasts are barely done. If there is time, let the chicken cool in the broth. Remove the chicken, strain the broth, then spoon off all the fat that rises to the top.

Heat a medium-sized skillet over medium-low heat for several minutes, then pour in the pumpkin seeds in a single layer. When the first one pops, stir them constantly for 4 to 5 minutes, until all have toasted and popped. Cool completely. In batches, pulverize the seeds in a spice grinder (or in a blender fitted with a miniblend container). Sift through a medium-mesh sieve, then stir in one cup of the broth.

If you have fresh tomatillos, simmer them with the whole chiles in salted water and cover until tender, 10 to 15 minutes. Drain and place in a blender or food processor. Simply drain canned tomatillos and place in the blender or food processor with the raw chiles. Tear the lettuce leaves into rough pieces and add to the tomatillos along with the onion, garlic, and fresh coriander. Pulverize the spices in a mortar or spice grinder, add to the blender, then process the mixture until smooth.

Heat the lard or oil in a large saucepan over medium heat. When hot, add the pumpkinseed-broth mixture and stir constantly for about 4 to 5 minutes until it thickens and darkens. Add the vegetable purée and stir a few minutes longer, until very thick. Stir in 2 cups of the chicken broth, reduce the heat to medium low, and simmer, partially covered, for about 30 minutes. For a smooth sauce, scrape this mixture into a blender jar, cover loosely and blend until smooth, then return to the saucepan. Season with salt and, if necessary, thin to a light consistency with a little broth.

Just before serving, add the chicken to the simmering sauce. When heated through, remove the breasts to a warm serving platter. Spoon the sauce over the breasts and decorate with sprigs of coriander.

Serves 4.

*Available at Mexican grocery stores.

FRONTERA GRILL
445 N. Clark Street
Chicago, Illinois 60610
(312) 661-1434

Chicken Breasts Moroccan Style

2 large chicken breasts, skinned,
   boned, and cut in half
4 tablespoons olive oil
1 cup chopped yellow onions
1 large clove garlic, minced
1 pound ripe plum tomatoes,
   peeled and diced
1 teaspoon turmeric
1 teaspoon grated fresh ginger,
   or ½ teaspoon powdered
   ginger

Cayenne pepper
Freshly ground black pepper
2½ cups chicken broth,
   preferably homemade
¾ cup green or Spanish salad
   olives, sliced, soaked
   in water, and rinsed well
   to desalt
Grated zest of ½ lemon
1 tablespoon minced parsley
1 tablespoon minced cilantro

In a large skillet, heat the olive oil. Sauté the chicken breasts for approximately 2 minutes on each side. Transfer the chicken to a plate.

Lower the heat to medium and add the chopped onions to the skillet. Sauté until lightly browned. Add the minced garlic and sauté a minute longer. Add the diced tomatoes and sauté for 2 to 3 minutes more, stirring to blend the ingredients. Add the turmeric and grated ginger. Season with cayenne and black pepper to taste. Stir for a minute to blend the flavors.

Add the 2½ cups of chicken broth. Raise the heat, stirring to reduce the sauce by one third. Add the chicken breasts to the sauce and cook for a minute longer. Add the rinsed olives and lemon zest and heat through for a minute. Add the minced parsley and minced cilantro. Mix lightly. Serve over rice if desired.

Serves 2 to 3.

CASBAH
514 W. Diversey
Chicago, Illinois 60614
(312) 935-7570

Smothered Chicken

1 frying chicken, 3 to 3½ pounds,
    cut into serving pieces
½ cup olive oil or vegetable oil
¾ cup evaporated milk
    combined with ¾ cup water
1 cup flour seasoned with 1
    teaspoon each salt and
    pepper
1 small yellow onion, sliced
1 large garlic clove, sliced
4 celery stalks, chopped
1 medium-sized carrot, peeled
    and chopped
1½ cups hot chicken stock,
    preferably homemade

Preheat the oven to 350°.

Wash the chicken pieces and dry thoroughly. Heat the oil in a large skillet until hot but not smoking. Dip the chicken pieces into the milk and water mixture. Then roll each piece in the seasoned flour, coating evenly. Shake off any excess flour. Brown the chicken rapidly, several pieces at a time, without cooking through.

Place the vegetables in a casserole large enough to accommodate both the vegetables and the chicken without crowding. Arrange the chicken pieces on top of the vegetables. Pour in the hot chicken stock and cover the casserole. Bake for 1½ hours, or until the chicken is tender.

Serves 4.

ARMY & LOU'S
420-22 E. 75th Street
Chicago, Illinois 60619
(312) 483-6550

Szechwan Hot Diced Chicken

For the seasoning sauce:
2 tablespoons soy sauce
1 tablespoon sugar
½ teaspoon salt
1 teaspoon sesame oil
1 tablespoon dry sherry
1 teaspoon cornstarch

For the Szechwan chicken:
1 pound boneless, skinned
    chicken breasts
1 tablespoon soy sauce
1½ tablespoons cornstarch
6 tablespoons vegetable oil
½ cup skinless raw peanuts

6 to 8 dried red peppers, whole
1 teaspoon fresh chopped ginger
½ cup diced green bell pepper
½ cup diced red bell pepper
½ cup green onions, white part
    only, cut into ¼-inch slices

To prepare the seasoning sauce:
In a small bowl, mix the soy sauce, sugar, salt, sesame oil, sherry, and cornstarch. Set aside.

To prepare the Szechwan chicken:
Cut the chicken breasts into 1-inch cubes and place in a bowl. Add the soy sauce and the cornstarch. Stir evenly in one direction until the chicken is well coated. Set aside for 30 minutes.

Heat 1 tablespoon of vegetable oil in a wok or saucepan. Sauté the peanuts until golden. Let cool.

Heat 3 tablespoons of vegetable oil in a wok or skillet until hot but not smoking. Add the chicken and stir-fry for 2 minutes. Remove the chicken and drain thoroughly.

Heat 2 tablespoons of vegetable oil in a wok or saucepan. Fry the dried red peppers until they turn black. (Break the peppers up if you prefer a spicier dish.) Add the ginger, green and red bell peppers, green onions, and chicken. Stir-fry quickly. Add the seasoning sauce, stirring until the mixture thickens and is heated thoroughly. Turn off the heat. Add the peanuts and mix well. Serve with steamed white rice.

Serves 4.

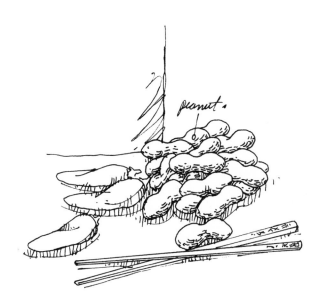

PINE YARD
924 Church Street
Evanston, Illinois 60201
(312) 475-4940

Chicken Toscano

2 frying chickens, about
　　2½ pounds each,
　　cut into serving pieces
1 small yellow onion,
　　finely chopped
1 stalk celery, finely chopped
4 teaspoons salt
3 teaspoons freshly ground
　　pepper, or to taste
½ teaspoon dried rosemary
　　leaves, crushed
3 cups water
1½ cups tomato purée

Preheat the oven to 375°.

Place the chicken pieces in one layer in 1 or 2 baking pans. Mix the onion, celery, salt, pepper, rosemary, water, and tomato purée together. Pour over the chicken.

Cover the baking pans and bake for about 1 hour. When you can pierce the chicken easily with a fork, uncover and bake an additional 15 minutes.

Serves 4 to 6.

TOSCANO
2439 S. Oakley Avenue
Chicago, Illinois 60608
(312) 376-4841

Chicken Vesuvio

*2 frying chickens, about
    2 1/2 pounds each
4 large red potatoes
Salt
Freshly ground pepper
1/4 cup virgin olive oil
1/4 cup freshly squeezed
    lemon juice
1 tablespoon fresh rosemary
    leaves
2 teaspoons minced garlic*

Cut each chicken into eight pieces. Rinse the chicken pieces well and dry thoroughly. Scrub and quarter each potato without peeling. Place the chicken and potatoes in a casserole. Season all with salt and pepper to taste. Drizzle the olive oil and lemon juice over the chicken and potatoes. Then sprinkle with the rosemary and garlic. Marinate in the refrigerator for at least 30 minutes, turning occasionally.

Preheat the oven to 425°. Bake the chicken for about 30 minutes. The chicken is done when the skin has browned and the juices run clear.

Serves 4 to 6.

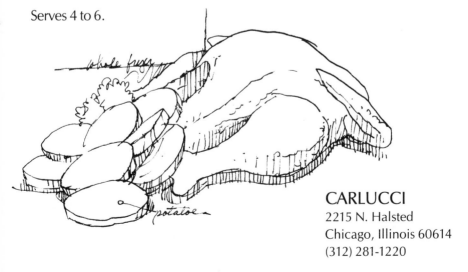

CARLUCCI
2215 N. Halsted
Chicago, Illinois 60614
(312) 281-1220

Voodoo Chicken

For the chicken:
3/4 teaspoon salt
3/4 teaspoon ground red pepper
1/2 teaspoon black pepper
1/4 teaspoon oregano
1/4 teaspoon thyme
1/4 teaspoon garlic powder
1/4 teaspoon white pepper
1/8 teaspoon rubbed sage,
    not ground
Vegetable oil
2 1/4 pounds boneless chicken
    breast, skinned and split

For the stuffing:
2 tablespoons unsalted butter
2 tablespoons margarine
2 cups chopped yellow onion
1 cup chopped celery
1 cup chopped green bell pepper
1/4 cup chopped green onion
1/4 cup chopped parsley

1 tablespoon minced garlic
1 tablespoon Tabasco sauce
1 pound boudin or andouille
    sausage, removed
    from casing
1 cup chicken stock,
    preferably homemade

For the red pepper hollandaise:
2 sticks unsalted butter
4 tablespoons margarine
2 red bell peppers, roasted,
    peeled, seeded, and puréed
1 fresh jalapeño pepper, chopped
1/8 cup water
2 egg yolks
1/2 tablespoon chopped parsley
1/2 tablespoon freshly squeezed
    lemon juice
1/4 teaspoon Tabasco sauce
1/4 teaspoon Worcestershire sauce

To prepare the chicken:
Combine the salt, red and black peppers, oregano, thyme, garlic powder,
white pepper, and sage and mix well. Coat the chicken with vegetable
oil and sprinkle evenly with the seasoning mixture. Grill, broil, or pan-
blacken the chicken until done.

To prepare the stuffing:
Preheat the oven to 375°.

Melt the butter and margarine in a large skillet over high heat. Add the
yellow onion, celery, and green pepper. Sauté until tender, about 10
minutes. Stir in the green onion, parsley, garlic, and Tabasco sauce and
continue cooking for 10 minutes, stirring occasionally. Reduce the heat
to medium and add the sausage. Cook for about 5 minutes, stirring
occasionally until the sausage breaks apart completely. Stir in the stock

and bring to a simmer. Continue cooking until the moisture is absorbed and the mixture thickens to the consistency of stuffing. Transfer the stuffing to an ungreased baking dish and bake, uncovered, for about 20 to 30 minutes until browned on top, stirring once during baking.

To prepare the red pepper hollandaise:
Melt the butter and the margarine in a small saucepan. Reserve and keep warm. In the top of a double boiler, combine the puréed peppers and chopped jalapeños, the water, egg yolks, parsley, lemon juice, Tabasco, and Worcestershire. Whisk continuously over simmering water until the mixture is thick and creamy. Gradually whip in the warm butter-margarine mixture, a little at a time. Keep warm.

To serve, place ½ cup of the stuffing on a dinner plate. Lay a chicken breast on top of the stuffing. Ladle ¼ cup of the pepper hollandaise sauce on top of the chicken.

Serves 6.

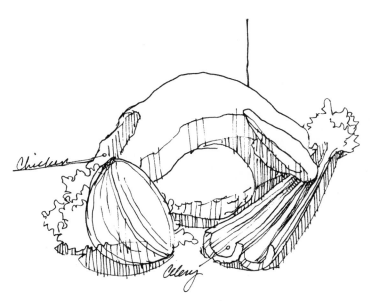

DIXIE BAR & GRILL
225 W. Chicago Avenue
Chicago, Illinois 60610
(312) 642-3336

Poulet Sauté aux Poireaux et Crème de Basilic

(Sautéed Chicken with Leeks and Basil Cream Sauce)

3 chickens, approximately
  2 pounds each, cut
  into serving pieces
  and boned (Your butcher
  can do this for you.)
3 tablespoons unsalted butter
1 pound leeks, cleaned
  and julienned
2 tablespoons chopped shallots
½ cup cognac

1 cup dry white wine
3 cups chicken stock,
  preferably homemade
2 cups heavy cream
1 tomato, peeled, seeded,
  and diced
10 fresh basil leaves, chopped
Salt
Freshly ground black pepper

Preheat oven to 400°. Melt the butter in a skillet over medium-high heat. Briefly sauté the chicken in batches without cooking through. Transfer the chicken to a casserole, leaving the butter and pan juices in the skillet. Bake the chicken for 15 minutes. Remove the chicken from the oven and set aside.

Sauté the julienne of leek in the pan juices—butter mixture for 5 minutes and remove. Sauté the shallots until transparent. Remove and set aside.

Add the cognac to the pan, flame, and reduce to a syrup. Add the white wine and reduce to a glaze. Add the chicken stock and reduce to ¼ cup. Add the cream and boil for 2 minutes. Add the diced tomato, basil, leeks, and shallots. Season to taste with salt and pepper. Nap the chicken with the sauce and serve.

Serves 6.

LE TITI DE PARIS
1015 W. Dundee Road
Arlington Heights, Illinois 60004
(312) 506-0222

Mustard Coated Confit of Duck on Greens

4 legs of duck confit
2 tablespoons Dijon mustard or
    Moutarde de Meaux
2 cups fine, fresh breadcrumbs
2 tablespoons sherry vinegar
Salt
Pepper
2 tablespoons chopped shallot
1 tablespoon walnut or
    hazelnut oil

2 to 4 tablespoons duck glaze
    (optional)
4 cups of specialty greens, such
    as red oak leaf, arugula,
    mache, frisee, radicchio,
    Belgian endive, and
    watercress, rinsed, dried, and
    torn into bite-sized pieces
4 tablespoons mixed fresh herbs
    of your choice

Preheat the oven to 400°.

Put the duck confit on a baking sheet. Brush the tops with the mustard and sprinkle the breadcrumbs generously on each. Bake for about 10 to 15 minutes until the duck is crisp and heated through.

While the duck is baking, make a simple vinaigrette by combining the sherry vinegar, salt and pepper to taste, and the shallots. Whisk in the oil. If desired, add the duck glaze to the vinaigrette by tablespoons until a rich flavor is achieved. Taste the vinaigrette as you make it.

After removing the duck from the oven, toss the greens and herbs with the vinaigrette. Divide the greens among 4 plates. Place one duck leg on top of each plate of greens and serve immediately.

Serves 4.

CAFÉ PROVENÇAL
1625 Hinman Avenue
Evanston, Illinois 60201
(312) 475-2233

Meat

Basil Beef

4 tablespoons vegetable oil
3 cloves garlic, minced
3 hot peppers, sliced
1 pound flank steak, thinly sliced
1/4 pound fresh mushrooms,
     sliced
2 to 3 tablespoons
     fish sauce*
1 tablespoon mushroom
     soy sauce* (optional)
1 teaspoon sugar
1/4 teaspoon white pepper
1/4 cup fresh basil

Heat the oil in a frying pan or wok over high heat. Add the garlic and sauté briefly. Add the hot peppers and stir a few times. Add the flank steak and mushrooms. Sauté for several minutes, stirring frequently. Add the fish sauce, optional mushroom soy sauce, sugar, white pepper, and basil. Cook until the beef is medium rare. Serve over steamed white rice.

Serves 4.

*Available at Oriental grocery stores.

RIVER KWAI
440 N. State Street
Chicago, Illinois 60610
(312) 644-1144

Garlic Tenderloin

1 pound beef tenderloin, cut into
    thin strips 3 inches long by
    ¼ inch wide
Flour to dust
2 tablespoons sesame oil
1 cup pea pods, trimmed
¾ cup diced yellow onion
¾ cup sliced mushrooms
1 cup fresh bean sprouts
½ cup raw cashews
1 medium red bell pepper, cored,
    seeded, and sliced into thin
    strips
2 cloves garlic, chopped
Water chestnuts (optional)
¾ cup oyster sauce combined
    with ¾ cup water*
Steamed rice
Green onion, chopped, for
    garnish

Lightly dust the beef with flour. Heat a wok or skillet until very hot. Add
the oil. Add all the ingredients up to and including the water chestnuts.
Stir vigorously until the meat is brown and the vegetables are thoroughly
heated. Add the oyster sauce and water to the mixture in the skillet. Bring
to a brisk boil. Stir. Pour over steamed rice and garnish with green onion.

Serves 4.

*Available at Oriental grocery stores.

PERIWINKLE
2511 N. Lincoln Avenue
Chicago, Illinois 60614
(312) 883-9797

Beef Lega Tibs

For the Berbere sauce:
1 teaspoon ground cardamon
    seeds
½ teaspoon cumin
1 teaspoon coriander
½ teaspoon cinnamon
¼ cup cayenne pepper
½ cup paprika
2 teaspoons finely minced
    red onion
3 teaspoons garlic powder
½ teaspoon ground ginger
2 teaspoons vegetable oil
Water

For the Lega Tibs:
2 tablespoons unsalted butter
⅓ cup chopped yellow onion
1 jalapeño pepper, stemmed,
    seeded, and chopped
3 pounds beef tenderloin, flank
    steak, or sirloin
3 teaspoons Berbere sauce
    (see below)
Rosemary, dried
Salt

To prepare the Berbere sauce:
Preheat the oven to 350°. Spread the cardamon, cumin, coriander, and cinnamon on a cookie sheet and roast in the oven for 2 to 3 minutes. Mix the roasted spices in a bowl with the cayenne pepper, paprika, red onion, garlic powder, and ginger. Add the vegetable oil and enough water to make a paste. Set aside.

To prepare the Lega Tibs:
Melt the butter in a skillet over medium-high heat. Sauté the onion and the jalapeño pepper until tender. Add the beef and 3 teaspoons of Berbere sauce. Sauté the beef on all sides until it reaches the degree of doneness you desire. Add a pinch of rosemary and salt to taste. Serve with *ingera* (unleavened, pancake-like bread) or pita bread.

Note: The Berbere sauce keeps well. Store it in a tightly covered jar in the refrigerator, and use it to flavor other dishes such as stews and stir-fries.

Serves 6.

MAMA DESTA'S RED SEA
3218 N. Clark Street
Chicago, Illinois 60657
(312) 935-7561

Punjene Paprike-Babure
(Stuffed Green Peppers)

3 tablespoons vegetable oil
1 large yellow onion, chopped
¼ cup uncooked rice
1 pound ground beef
½ pound ground veal
1 tablespoon fresh chopped
    parsley
1 egg

Salt
Freshly ground black pepper
Paprika
8 green bell peppers, cored and
    seeded (Do not cut peppers
    into halves.)
5 fresh tomatoes, sliced
1 tablespoon flour

Preheat the oven to 350°.

Heat the 3 tablespoons of vegetable oil in a large skillet. Sauté the onion until translucent. Add the raw rice, ground beef, and ground veal. Sauté until the meat is browned. Off heat, add the parsley and egg. Add salt, pepper, and paprika to taste.

Fill each pepper with the sautéed mixture. Cover the openings of the bell peppers with one slice of tomato. Oil an oven-proof dish. Add ¼ inch of water to the dish. Mix 1 tablespoon of flour into the water. Place the stuffed peppers in the dish and surround with the remaining tomatoes. Bake in the oven for 45 minutes to an hour, adding a little water from time to time as needed.

Serves 8.

YUGO INN
2824 N. Ashland
Chicago, Illinois 60657
(312) 548-6444

Beef Rouladen

For the brown sauce:
1¼ pounds veal or chicken bones
4 tablespoons vegetable oil
½ carrot, sliced
½ rib of celery, chopped
½ yellow onion, chopped
1 clove garlic, chopped
4 tablespoons flour
1 quart beef stock or bouillon
¾ bay leaf
2 peppercorns
¼ cup tomato purée
⅛ cup chopped tomatoès

3 tablespoons mustard,
    Dusseldorf style
¼ cup milk
¼ cup breadcrumbs
1 tablespoon chopped
    fresh parsley
1 teaspoon salt
1 teaspoon freshly ground
    black pepper
4 thin slices round of beef
4 thin strips sour pickle
2 tablespoons margarine
2 cups homemade brown sauce

For the rouladen:
2 strips bacon, diced
½ pound ground beef
½ cup chopped yellow onion
1 clove fresh garlic, chopped
2 eggs

To prepare the brown sauce:
Brown the bones in the oil. Add the carrot, celery, onion, and garlic, and
braise them until light brown. Add the flour, stir well, and cook until the
flour turns brown, stirring so that it browns evenly. Add the beef stock.
Add the bay leaf, peppercorns, tomato purée, and chopped tomatoes.
Bring to a boil. Then reduce the heat and let simmer slowly for 3 to 4
hours. Strain.

To prepare the rouladen:
Preheat the oven to 325°.

In a medium sauté pan, sauté the bacon, ground beef, onion, and garlic
until lightly browned. Let cool. Place the sautéed mixture in a large
mixing bowl and add the eggs, mustard, milk, breadcrumbs, parsley,
salt, and pepper. Mix well.

Spread the mixture on the four slices of beef. Place a pickle strip on top of the mixture and then roll up each beef slice. Secure with toothpicks or tie with a string. Melt the margarine in a sauté pan over medium heat and brown the roulades on all sides. Place the roulades in a baking pan and cover with the hot brown sauce. Bake at 325° until tender, approximately 1½ to 2 hours.

Serves 4.

ZUM DEUTSCHEN ECK
2924 N. Southport
Chicago, Illinois 60657
(312) 525-8121

Beef Tenderloin à la Deutsch

2 tablespoons unsalted butter
2 yellow onions, diced
2 cloves garlic
2 green bell peppers, cored,
    seeded, and diced
12 mushrooms, sliced
1½ cups red wine (burgundy)
1 quart brown sauce
    (See Beef Rouladen,
    pages 108–109)

2 tablespoons vegetable oil
1½ pounds beef tenderloin, cut
    into ¼-inch-thick slices
    (round steak or sirloin steak
    can be substituted)
Salt
Freshly ground black pepper
2 tomatoes, peeled, seeded,
    and chopped

Melt the butter in a large skillet or Dutch oven over medium heat. Sauté the onions, garlic, and green peppers. Add the mushrooms and ¾ of the wine. Reduce the mixture by ½ and add the brown sauce. Cook until the vegetables are al dente.

Heat the oil in a large skillet over high heat. Sauté the beef tenderloin quickly on both sides until well browned. Season well with salt and pepper. Drain the excess fat and add the brown sauce mixture. Bring the sauce to a boil, reduce the heat, and simmer slowly until the vegetables are tender, about 1¼ to 1½ hours. Add the remaining wine and tomatoes and serve.

Serves 4.

ZUM DEUTSCHEN ECK
2924 N. Southport
Chicago, Illinois 60657
(312) 525-8121

Gosht Vindaloo   *(Indian Spicy Beef Stew)*

1 onion, coarsely chopped
3 garlic cloves, peeled
2 tablespoons coriander seeds
1 tablespoon turmeric
2 teaspoons red pepper flakes
1 teaspoon powdered ginger
½ teaspoon cumin seeds
½ teaspoon fenugreek seeds*
½ teaspoon mustard seeds
¼ cup red wine vinegar
4 tablespoons unsalted butter
2 pounds stewing beef, trimmed
    of all fat and cut into
    1-inch cubes

Put the onion, garlic, coriander seeds, turmeric, red pepper flakes, ginger, cumin seeds, fenugreek seeds, and mustard seeds in a blender. Blend, adding enough vinegar to make a thick paste.

Put the meat in a large bowl and coat well with the paste. Marinate at least 4 hours or preferably overnight.

Melt the butter in a wok or heavy skillet. Add the beef along with the marinade paste and brown the beef over high heat. Then lower the flame and simmer until tender, about 1½ hours, stirring occasionally. Serve with rice.

Serves 6 to 8.

*Available at Indian grocery stores.

BOMBAY PALACE
50 E. Walton
Chicago, Illinois 60611
(312) 664-9323

Señoritas *(Stuffed Potato Shells)*

6 medium-sized baking potatoes

For the chicken stuffing:
½ chicken breast
3 cloves garlic, minced
¼ cup chopped Spanish onion
1 cup good quality tomato sauce

For the beef stuffing:
1 tablespoon corn oil
¼ cup chopped Spanish onion
1 clove garlic, minced
½ green bell pepper, diced
6 ounces ground beef
Freshly ground black pepper
1 medium-sized tomato, peeled,
    seeded, and diced
Salt

For the shrimp stuffing:
12 medium shrimp, peeled
    and deveined

½ lime
¼ cup chopped Spanish onion

For the guacamole stuffing:
1 ripe avocado
1 medium-sized tomato, peeled,
    seeded, and diced
¼ cup chopped Spanish onion
Salt

For the Señoritas:
½ head iceberg or leaf lettuce,
    shredded
3 medium-sized tomatoes,
    peeled, seeded, and diced
1 large Spanish onion, diced
1 bunch fresh cilantro, chopped
4 jalapeño peppers, seeded
    and chopped
1 cup sour cream

To prepare the potatoes:
Preheat the oven to 350°. Scrub each potato well, wrap in aluminum foil, and bake for 1 hour or until tender. While the potatoes are baking, prepare the stuffings. When the potatoes are done, cut them into halves and scoop out the centers, leaving about ¼ inch of potato and skin.

To prepare the chicken stuffing:
Boil the chicken breast with the garlic and onion in enough water to cover for about 15 minutes. When cool, remove the skin, fat, and bone. Shred the chicken into very small pieces. Add the chicken pieces to the tomato sauce. Set aside.

To prepare the beef stuffing:
Heat the corn oil in a skillet. Briefly sauté the onion, garlic, and bell pepper. Add the ground beef and a pinch of black pepper. Sauté for 5 minutes. Then add the tomato. Mix well and salt to taste.

To prepare the shrimp stuffing:
Drop the shrimp into a pot of boiling water containing the lime and onion. Cook for 1 minute, then drain the shrimp and place into tepid water immediately. Drain again, then shred the shrimp.

To prepare the guacamole stuffing:
Cut the avocado in half, remove the pit, and scoop the pulp from the skin. Mash the pulp until it has a smooth, creamy consistency. Add the tomatoes, onion, and salt to taste. Mix thoroughly.

To assemble the Señoritas:
Spread shredded lettuce on 4 serving plates and center 3 potato halves on each plate. On the first plate, fill one potato half with equal amounts of chicken and guacamole. Top with chopped tomatoes, chopped onion, and cilantro. Fill another potato half with equal portions of beef stuffing and guacamole, topping with tomatoes, onion, and cilantro. Then fill the third potato half with the shrimp stuffing and guacamole. Again, top with tomatoes, onion, and cilantro. Repeat for the potato halves on the other 3 plates. With each serving, include a small dish of chopped jalapeños and a small bowl of sour cream.

Serves 4.

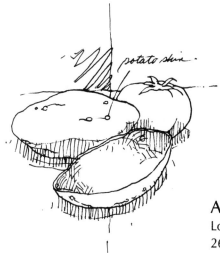

potato skin

ABRIL
Logan Square
2607 N. Milwaukee Avenue
Chicago, Illinois 60647
(312) 227-7252

Lamb Lou

1 tablespoon olive oil
1 tablespoon sesame oil
2 large cloves garlic, minced
6 large Kum Pow peppers*
1 tablespoon white sesame seeds
3/4 tablespoon crushed anise
    seeds
1/2 teaspoon coarsely ground
    black pepper
1 teaspoon sassafras powder**
1 teaspoon paprika
1 teaspoon freshly squeezed
    lemon juice
1 teaspoon orange juice
1 teaspoon Chinese black
    vinegar*

1 teaspoon soy sauce
1 1/2 teaspoons fresh thyme
    (or 1/4 teaspoon dried)
2 pounds thinly sliced lamb
    scallopine, cut from the leg
    and fully trimmed
1 each poblano, red bell, and
    yellow bell peppers, cored,
    seeded, and cut into
    1/3-inch-wide strips***
1 teaspoon Ricard or Pernod liquer
1 tablespoon coarsely chopped
    parsley

Heat the olive oil and the sesame oil in a sauté pan over medium heat.
Sauté the garlic and Kum Pow peppers until the garlic turns golden. Add
the sesame seeds, anise seeds, black pepper, sassafras powder, and
paprika, and stir for a few seconds. Add the lemon juice, orange juice,
vinegar, soy sauce, and thyme. Remove from heat and allow to cool.
Lightly pound each scallopine to flatten. Add the lamb to the cooled
marinade and marinate, refrigerated, for at least 2 hours.

Preheat the oven to 200°. Remove the lamb from the marinade and
reserve the remaining marinade. Heat a large, heavy sauté pan over high
heat for 3 minutes. (Pan must be very hot.) Quickly sear the scallopine in
batches in the dry sauté pan. Sear for just a few seconds on each side so
that the interior of each scallopine remains rare. As the scallopine are
done, remove to a heat-proof platter and hold in the warm oven.

When all the lamb has been seared, add the marinade, pepper strips, and Ricard or Pernod to the sauté pan. Sauté quickly. When the peppers are barely cooked, return the lamb to the pan and toss with the peppers just long enough to heat through. Toss with the parsley and serve.

Serves 6.

*Available at Chinese markets.
**Available at health food stores.
***Poblano peppers are available at Mexican grocery stores.

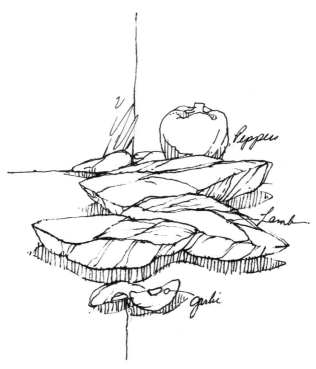

STAR TOP CAFÉ
2748 N. Lincoln Avenue
Chicago, Illinois 60614
(312) 281-0997

Irish Lamb Stew

2 pounds cubed lamb shoulder,
    trimmed
1 gallon water
½ tablespoon salt
1 tablespoon chicken base
1¼ teaspoons freshly ground
    black pepper
¼ teaspoon MSG (optional)
2 cups coarsely diced carrots
2 cups coarsely diced celery

1 leek, trimmed, rinsed
    thoroughly, and thinly sliced
3 medium green bell peppers,
    cored, seeded, and diced
1 jar (16 ounces) sweet, white,
    whole onions
1 can (16 ounces) Irish potatoes
½ pound (2 sticks) unsalted butter
¾ cup all-purpose flour

Add the lamb shoulder to 2 quarts of water and bring to a boil. When the water comes to a boil, pour it off. Add 2 more quarts of water to the lamb along with the salt, chicken base, ground pepper, and MSG. Bring to a boil. Then add the carrots, celery, leek, and green pepper. Reduce heat and simmer for 20 minutes. Add the onions and potatoes. Simmer for another 10 to 15 minutes or until the lamb is tender.

Melt the butter in a saucepan over medium heat. Stir in the flour and cook for several minutes, stirring constantly. Do not let the butter and flour mixture color. Remove the meat and vegetables from their broth. Add the butter and flour mixture to the broth and stir over medium heat until the broth thickens—about 10 minutes. Return the meat and vegetables to the sauce, simmer until heated through, and serve.

Serves 6.

BINYON'S
327 S. Plymouth Court
Chicago, Illinois 60604
(312) 341-1155

Carne de Puerco con Calabazas
(Pork Stew with Zucchini)

3 pounds lean pork, trimmed and
    cut into 1-inch cubes
1 cup water
Salt
Freshly ground black pepper
2 pounds zucchini, cut into
    ½-inch cubes
6 ripe tomatoes, seeded
    and diced
2 medium onions, sliced
6 poblano peppers, cored,
    seeded, and cut into strips*
1 cup tomato sauce

In a Dutch oven, simmer the pork in the water for about 30 minutes. Add salt and pepper to taste. When the water has evaporated and the pork is tender, add the zucchini, tomatoes, onions, poblano peppers, and tomato sauce. Cover tightly and simmer for about an hour. Serve with Spanish rice.

Serves 8.

*Available at Mexican grocery stores.

EL JARDIN
3335 N. Clark Street
Chicago, Illinois 60657
(312) 528-6775

Coconut Pork

2 tablespoons vegetable oil
5 slices fresh ginger, peeled and
    sliced into matchsticks
4 cloves garlic, minced
3 dried chili peppers
1 pound lean pork, sliced into thin
    strips
1 teaspoon salt
4 teaspoons sugar
1 teaspoon soy sauce
1 can (14 ounces) Thai coconut
    milk (not Hawaiian)*

Heat the oil in a skillet or a wok. Add the ginger, garlic, and chili peppers.
Crush the peppers if you prefer a hotter, spicier sauce. Cook until the
garlic is golden. Add the sliced pork. Stir and cook until the pork turns
white. Add the salt, sugar, and soy sauce. Add the coconut milk and
bring to a boil. Simmer for at least 20 minutes or until the pork is tender.
Serve with rice if desired.

Serves 4.

*Available at Oriental grocery stores.

HUÉ
1138 W. Argyle
Chicago, Illinois 60640
(312) 275-4044

Masitas de Puerco *(Morsels of Fried Pork)*

3 pounds pork, boneless
¾ cup lemon juice,
    freshly squeezed
2 tablespoons salt
½ teaspoon ground pepper
2 teaspoons ground cumin
1 tablespoon oregano
1 clove garlic, mashed
2 cups vegetable oil

Cut the pork into ¾-inch squares. Marinate the pork pieces in the lemon juice, salt, pepper, cumin, oregano, and garlic for about two hours.

Drain the pork and pat dry with a paper towel. Heat the oil in a large pan or deep fryer until hot but not smoking, about 350°. Deep fry the pork in small batches until golden, about 1 minute. Serve with white rice, black beans, and tortillas.

Serves 4.

TANIA'S
2659 N. Milwaukee Avenue
Chicago, Illinois 60647
(312) 235-6797

Szechwan Spicy Pork with Wood Ears and Water Chestnuts

10 ounces pork tenderloin
2 tablespoons soy sauce, divided
4 teaspoons cornstarch, divided
2 tablespoons wood ears*
1 tablespoon vinegar
1 tablespoon hot pepper oil,
      or to taste**
½ cup dry white wine or sherry
1 teaspoon sugar
½ teaspoon salt
1 teaspoon sesame oil
1 tablespoon chopped
      green onion
5 tablespoons vegetable oil,
      2 tablespoons reserved
1 teaspoon chopped garlic
6 to 8 water chestnuts,
      finely chopped
2 tablespoons bamboo shoots

Cut the pork tenderloin into long thin slices. Marinate in 1 tablespoon soy sauce and 2 teaspoons cornstarch for 20 minutes.

Soak the wood ears in warm water until soft. Rinse well and cut into small slices.

To prepare the seasoning sauce:
In a small bowl, combine 1 tablespoon of soy sauce, the vinegar, hot pepper oil, wine or sherry, sugar, salt, 2 teaspoons of the cornstarch, sesame oil, and the green onion. Stir well.

To prepare the pork:
Heat 3 tablespoons of the vegetable oil in a large skillet or wok. Place the pork in the skillet or wok and stir-fry for 30 seconds to 1 minute. Remove the pork. Drain the oil.

Heat the remaining 2 tablespoons of vegetable oil in the skillet or wok. Add the garlic and stir. Add the water chestnuts and bamboo shoots and stir for 30 seconds. Then add the pork, stirring thoroughly. Add the seasoning sauce and stir-fry for a few more seconds. Serve with white rice.

Serves 2 to 3.

*Wood ears are dehydrated mushrooms and are available at Oriental grocery stores.
**Hot pepper oil is also available at Oriental groceries. It is very hot, and the amount may be decreased to taste.

PINE YARD
924 Church Street
Evanston, Illinois 60201
(312) 475-4940

Pork Chops with Sun-Dried Tomatoes, Rosemary, and Walnuts

Leaves from 5 sprigs fresh rosemary,
    finely chopped
¼ cup sun-dried tomatoes in oil,
    drained and finely chopped
¼ cup finely chopped walnuts
6 center-cut pork chops,
    10 ounces each
2 tablespoons olive oil, plus
    more for brushing on the
    pork chops

Preheat the oven to 325°.

Combine the rosemary, sun-dried tomatoes, and walnuts to use as a breading mixture. Brush the chops lightly with olive oil. Pat the breading on the chops. Let the breaded pork chops sit for 10 minutes.

Heat 2 tablespoons of olive oil over medium heat in an ovenproof skillet large enough to hold the chops without crowding. Brown the pork chops on both sides. Turn the chops carefully so as not to dislodge the breading.

Finish cooking in the oven for 20 minutes.

Serves 6.

LE COCHONNET
3443 N. Sheffield
Chicago, Illinois 60657
(312) 525-5888

New Orleans Style Muffuletta

½ cup finely chopped fresh
    broccoli florets
½ cup finely chopped fresh
    cauliflower florets
½ cup finely chopped celery
1 cup pimiento-stuffed olives,
    finely chopped, with ¼ cup
    liquid from jar
4 cloves garlic, finely chopped
¼ cup extra virgin olive oil
¼ teaspoon freshly ground
    black pepper

2 lengths of French bread,
    6 inches each, or small
    round loaves
¼ pound Genoa salami,
    thinly sliced
¼ pound prosciutto,
    thinly sliced
¼ pound provolone cheese,
    thinly sliced

In a medium-sized bowl, combine the broccoli, cauliflower, celery, olives, olive juice, garlic, olive oil, and black pepper. Let this mixture stand for at least an hour.

Preheat the oven to 325°.

Slice each piece of bread or loaf in half horizontally. On each bottom half, spread the olive salad. Then alternate layers of salami, ham, and provolone, ending with a layer of provolone. To complete the sandwich, moisten the top half of the bread with the leftover liquid from the olive salad.

Bake the sandwiches for 15 to 20 minutes or until thoroughly warmed through. Remove the sandwiches from the oven, cut in half, and serve.

Serves 2.

R.S.V.P. & CO.
3324 N. Broadway
Chicago, Illinois 60657
(312) 975-1102

Calzone with Mushrooms, Onions, and Italian Sausage

¼ ounce (1 package) dry yeast
½ cup water, warmed to 100°
2 tablespoons whole wheat flour
1½ teaspoons honey
3½ cups bread flour
¼ teaspoon salt
1 tablespoon olive oil, plus more
    for brushing
⅞ cup water, warmed to 70°
¼ cup olive oil
4 large cloves garlic, minced
¼ teaspoon red pepper flakes
1 tablespoon dried oregano

1 can (28 ounces) imported Italian
    tomatoes, crushed
2 tablespoons tomato paste
Salt
2 tablespoons unsalted butter
1 pound fresh mushrooms,
    quartered
1 large onion, sliced
1 pound Italian sausage,
    removed from casing
2½ cups shredded
    mozzarella cheese

To prepare the dough:
Dissolve the yeast in the ½ cup warm water. In a bowl, mix ¼ cup of the yeast mixture with the whole wheat flour and the honey. (Discard the rest of the yeast.) Let this mixture sit in a warm place for 20 minutes.

Put the bread flour, salt, 1 tablespoon of olive oil, and ⅞ cup of warm water into the bowl of a mixer equipped with a dough hook. Add the yeast starter. Mix on low speed for 3 minutes (or knead by hand for 10 minutes). Divide the dough into 4 equal portions. Roll each portion into a round ball. Place the dough balls on a floured baking sheet about 4 inches apart. Brush the tops with olive oil. Cover the dough with plastic wrap and refrigerate for 3 hours or freeze for another day's use. (Thaw frozen dough in the refrigerator overnight.) Remove the dough balls from the refrigerator and let the dough come to room temperature. Lightly flour a pastry or cutting board and roll out each dough ball into a circle until it is about ⅛ inch thick.

To prepare the sauce:
Combine the ¼ cup of olive oil, garlic, pepper flakes, and oregano in a sauté pan and sauté slowly over medium heat for 2 minutes. Add the crushed tomatoes and simmer for another 20 minutes. Stir in the tomato paste. Add salt to taste.

To prepare the calzone:
Preheat the oven to 500°.

Melt the butter in a saucepan over medium heat, and briefly sauté the mushrooms and the onion. In a separate skillet, crumble and cook the sausage. Drain. Cover half of each of the dough circles with sauce, leaving a ½-inch border. Add the mushrooms, onion, sausage, and mozzarella cheese. Fold the uncovered half over the topping and crimp the edges together. Bake for 8 to 10 minutes. Serve immediately.

Serves 4.

Note: The calzone can be prepared with your choice of ingredients: green peppers, olives, anchovies, pepperoni, artichoke hearts, or shrimp, for example.

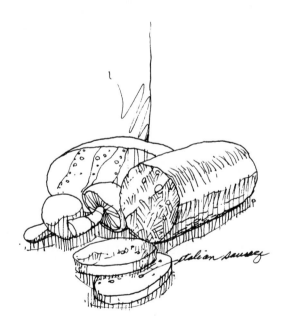

Italian sausage

SCOOZI!
410 W. Huron
Chicago, Illinois 60610
(312) 943-5900

Paella Valencia

1 cup olive oil
1 whole garlic clove, peeled
1 medium onion, finely chopped
1 green bell pepper, cored,
 seeded, and finely chopped
2 fresh tomatoes, peeled, seeded,
 and finely chopped
Chicken (about 2 pounds), cut
 into 12 serving pieces
1 pound lean boneless pork loin,
 cut into 1/2-inch cubes
3 links of chorizo, or substitute
 1/2 pound other garlic-
 seasoned, smoked pork
 sausage
3 medium-sized squid, cleaned
 (Cut the sacs into rings, but
 leave the tentacles whole.)
6 cups chicken stock,
 preferably homemade

1/4 teaspoon saffron threads
Salt
3 cups raw medium- or long-grain
 white rice or imported
 short-grain white rice
12 small clams
12 mussels, cleaned and soaked
12 medium raw shrimp in
 their shells
1/2 cup fresh or frozen peas
1 medium red bell pepper, cored,
 seeded, and cut into strips
1 clove garlic, mashed
2 tablespoons minced
 fresh parsley
1/4 cup dry white wine
2 lemons, cut into wedges

Use a 14-inch paella pan or a large skillet, 2- to 2½-inches deep. Set the pan or skillet on medium heat. When hot, add the olive oil, whole garlic clove, onion, and green pepper. Sauté until the vegetables are soft. Remove the garlic. Add the tomatoes, chicken, pork loin, sausage, and squid. Sauté for about 10 minutes.

Season the chicken stock with the saffron and salt to taste. Add the seasoned stock to the paella pan. Bring to a rapid boil. Add the rice, spreading evenly over the meat and stock mixture. Cook for 8 to 10 minutes.

Arrange the clams, mussels, and shrimp over the mixture in the pan.
Lower the heat and add the peas and red pepper strips. Add the mashed
garlic and parsley. Cook approximately 10 more minutes. Pour the wine
over the paella and cook for a few additional minutes. Let the paella rest
for 5 minutes and serve, garnished with lemon wedges.

Serves 6.

LA PAELLA
2920 N. Clark
Chicago, Illinois 60657
(312) 528-0757

Medallions of Veal with Candied Lemon Zest and Ginger

Peels, yellow part only, of 3 lemons, finely julienned
6 ounces fresh ginger root, peeled and finely julienned
1 cup water
1 cup sugar
1 quart Madeira
7 to 10 shallots, finely chopped (a handful)

2 cups veal stock
Salt
Pepper
6 tablespoons unsalted butter
6 veal medallions (approximately 2 ounces each), lightly pounded

In a saucepan, blanch the lemon zest and ginger in boiling water for 10 seconds. Drain and set aside. Bring 1 cup water and the sugar to a boil in a saucepan. Reduce to a syrup. Add the blanched ginger and lemon zest and cook for 5 minutes. Set aside.

Bring the Madeira and shallots to a boil in a saucepan. Cook for 45 minutes to an hour, reducing to a glaze. Add the veal stock. Strain the sauce. Add salt and pepper to taste. Swirl in 3 tablespoons of the butter to finish.

Sauté the veal in 3 tablespoons of butter over medium high heat, approximately 1½ minutes per side. Do not overcook. The medallions should be medium-rare to medium. Remove the medallions to warm plates, 2 per serving. Pour the sauce around the medallions and garnish with the candied lemon zest and ginger. Serve with fresh pasta.

Serves 3.

YOSHI'S CAFÉ
3257 N. Halsted
Chicago, Illinois 60657
(312) 248-6160

Veal Limone

2 pounds of veal scallops
Salt
White pepper
½ cup all-purpose flour
1 stick unsalted butter
Juice of 1 lemon, freshly squeezed
1 tablespoon chopped Italian
    parsley
½ cup dry white wine
Sliced lemon, for garnish

Pound the veal scallops until they are flat and then season with salt and pepper to taste. Flour the veal on one side only. Sauté on the floured side in batches, using 2 tablespoons of butter for each batch, until the veal turns white, about 45 to 60 seconds over medium-high heat. Return all the veal to the skillet, add the lemon juice, and sprinkle with parsley. Pour the wine over the veal, turn the heat up to high, and let the wine bubble for about two minutes. Arrange the veal on individual heated plates. Pour the pan juices over the veal, and garnish with a slice of lemon.

Serves 4 to 6.

COMO INN
546 N. Milwaukee Avenue
Chicago, Illinois 60622
(312) 421-5222

Medallions of Veal with Gorgonzola Cream Sauce

2 pounds veal medallions
Unsalted butter
1 tablespoon chopped fresh
  rosemary
1 tablespoon chopped thyme
1 bay leaf
1 cup dry white wine
1 ounce imported Gorgonzola
  cheese (or to taste), crumbled
½ quart whipping cream

Pound the medallions lightly to flatten. Sauté the veal in batches, using 2 tablespoons of butter for each batch. Sauté until the veal is white, about 30 to 45 seconds. Keep the veal warm while making the sauce.

Combine the rosemary, thyme, bay leaf, and white wine in a saucepan and boil over medium heat for approximately 10 minutes to reduce. Lower the heat and stir in the crumbled Gorgonzola until it melts. Add the whipping cream. Heat through but do not boil. Remove the bay leaf. Serve over the sautéed veal.

Serves 6.

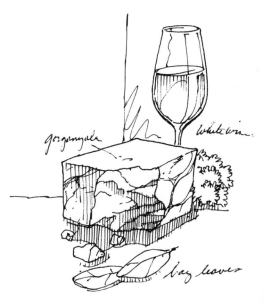

CONVITO ITALIANO
11 E. Chestnut Street
Chicago, Illinois 60611
(312) 943-2984

Ossobuco *(Braised Veal Shanks)*

For the veal:
3 tablespoons olive oil
4 veal shanks
2 tablespoons diced onion
2 tablespoons diced carrot
2 tablespoons diced celery
8 cups veal stock
2 bay leaves
Salt
Freshly ground black pepper

For the gremoulade:
4 fresh sage leaves
1 clove garlic
Peeled zest (yellow part only)
      of 1 lemon

To prepare the veal:
Preheat the oven to 350°.

Heat the oil in a deep, ovenproof skillet until very hot. Add the veal shanks and brown well on all sides. Add the onion, carrot, and celery, and sauté briefly. Add the veal stock, bay leaves, and salt and pepper to taste. Cover the skillet and place in the oven for 30 to 45 minutes or until the meat is very tender when pierced with a fork.

To prepare the gremoulade:
While the meat is cooking, finely mince the sage, garlic, and lemon zest and mix together. When the veal is tender, sprinkle it with the gremoulade and serve immediately.

Serves 4.

SPIAGGIA
980 N. Michigan Avenue
Chicago, Illinois 60611
(312) 280-2750

Veal Normande

For the herb mixture:
1 teaspoon freshly ground
    black pepper
3 bay leaves
½ teaspoon dried oregano
¼ teaspoon dried marjoram
¼ teaspoon dried savory
¼ teaspoon dried basil
¼ teaspoon dried thyme
¼ teaspoon dried rosemary

For the mirepoix:
1 tablespoon peanut oil
2 cloves garlic, crushed
1 cup finely diced celery
1 cup finely diced carrot
2 cups chopped yellow onion
2 teaspoons herb mixture
    (see preparation below)
¼ cup dry sherry

For the demiglace:
1 pound cracked veal bones
Mirepoix (see preparation below)
1 cup chicken stock,
    preferably homemade
1 cup dry white wine

For the Veal Normande:
1 pound veal medallions
    cut from the loin
Salt
White pepper
¼ pound clarified sweet butter

For the Sauce Normande:
¼ cup Calvados (apple brandy)
¼ cup veal demiglace
    (see preparation below)
¼ cup whipping cream

For garnish (optional):
½ apple, cored, peeled, and sliced
2 tablespoons clarified butter

To prepare the herb mixture:
Crush the black pepper, bay leaves, oregano, marjoram, savory, basil, thyme, and rosemary together.

To prepare the mirepoix:
Heat the peanut oil over medium heat. Sauté the garlic, celery, carrot, and onion for 3 minutes. Add 2 teaspoons of the herb blend, and sauté until the vegetables are not quite tender. Deglaze the pan by adding the sherry and stirring with a wooden spoon until the brown glaze formed on the bottom of the pan is liquefied. Cool and refrigerate.

To prepare the *demiglace:*
Combine the cracked veal bones in a roasting pan with the *mirepoix,* chicken stock, and white wine. Bake in a 250° oven for 24 hours. Strain, and reduce on the top of the stove for 2 hours.

To prepare the veal:
Pound the medallions until thin. Season with a pinch of salt and white pepper. Sauté in batches in a large skillet in clarified butter over medium heat for about 2 minutes per side until the veal turns white. Remove the veal and keep it warm.

To prepare the Sauce Normande:
With the Calvados, deglaze the pan in which you sautéed the veal. Add the ¼ cup veal *demiglace* and whipping cream. Stir together rapidly over high heat. Do not boil. Pour over the meat and serve immediately.

If desired, sauté the apple slices in the clarified butter and add to the Sauce Normande as a garnish for the veal.

Serves 4.

LA BOHÈME
566 Chestnut Street
Winnetka, Illinois 60093
(312) 446-4600

Chicken, Veal, and Parsley Pie

2 chicken breasts (8 ounces each),
    skinned and boned
2 cups chablis
6 to 8 tablespoons unsalted butter
1 large onion, diced
2 teaspoons salt
1 teaspoon white pepper
2 teaspoons fresh marjoram,
    diced, or ½ teaspoon dried
2 to 3 pounds veal, trimmed and
    cut into 1-inch cubes
1 cup parsley, packed then
    chopped
1 cup grated carrot
2 to 3 tablespoons flour
2 egg yolks
1 cup heavy cream
1 tablespoon Dijon mustard
Unsweetened pastry, homemade
    or frozen, enough to line
    6 individual baking dishes
1½ cups fresh breadcrumbs

Preheat the oven to 425°.

Place the chicken breasts in one layer in a large casserole. Add the chablis and cover the casserole. Braise the chicken breasts in the oven for about 15 minutes until firm and cooked through. When the chicken breasts are done, remove and chill them, reserving the braising liquid.

Melt 2 tablespoons of the butter in a heavy skillet over medium heat. Sauté the onion until translucent. Add the salt, pepper, and marjoram, and continue to sauté until the onion begins to brown lightly. Remove the onion to a large bowl. Melt 2 to 3 tablespoons of the butter in a large skillet over medium-high heat. Sauté the veal until it releases its juices and they run clear. The veal should still be slightly pink. Pour off the juices and combine them with the reserved braising liquid. Add the veal to the bowl with the onions. Cube the chilled chicken and add it to the veal and onions along with the chopped parsley and the grated carrot.

Add the remaining butter to the skillet and heat it to bubbling. Sprinkle on the flour and whisk for 2 minutes to cook the flour. Whisk in the reserved liquid and cook at a simmer until thickened. In a small bowl, combine the egg yolks, cream, and mustard. Whisk together well and add to the skillet, whisking for 1 minute more. Remove from the heat and add to the veal and vegetables. Combine well.

Line 6 individual baking dishes with pastry. Fill with the veal mixture, top with breadcrumbs (about 1/4 cup each), and bake until the mixture is bubbling around the edges and the crumbs are browned. Let settle for a few minutes before serving.

Serves 6.

WICKLINE'S
3335 N. Halsted
Chicago, Illinois 60657
(312) 525-4415

Spaghetti

Rice

linguine

Pasta, Rice, and Noodles

Pasta al'Olio *(Pasta with Garlic)*

½ cup olive oil
1 stick unsalted butter
4 tablespoons chopped fresh
    Italian parsley
½ cup chopped fresh garlic
Salt
Pepper
1 pound linguine
Imported Parmesan cheese,
    freshly grated

In a skillet, heat the olive oil and butter. Add the parsley, garlic, and salt and pepper to taste. Sauté until the garlic just begins to color.

Cook the linguine in a large pot of boiling, salted water until *al dente*. Drain well. Pour the sauce over the linguine. Serve with the freshly grated Parmesan cheese.

Serves 4.

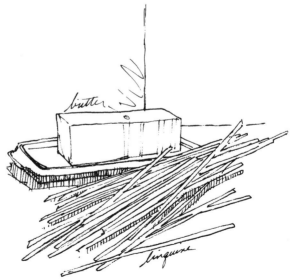

BACCHANALIA
2413 S. Oakley
Chicago, Illinois 60608
(312) 254-6555

Linguine Puttanesca

4 tablespoons extra virgin olive oil
4 cloves garlic, minced
½ medium yellow onion, minced
1 pound ripe tomatoes, peeled,
    seeded, and coarsely puréed
2 teaspoons capers
¼ pound Italian black olives,
    pitted and coarsely chopped
½ teaspoon hot red pepper flakes
4 anchovy fillets in oil, drained
    and mashed (optional)
1 pound linguine
Fresh parsley, minced
Fresh basil leaves

Heat the oil in a skillet. Add the garlic and onion and sauté until translucent. Add the tomatoes, capers, olives, red pepper flakes, and anchovies if desired. Bring the mixture to a simmer, and simmer for 15 minutes. When the sauce is ready, cook the linguine in a large pot of boiling, salted water until *al dente*. Drain the linguine and place it in a deep, warm platter. Pour the sauce over the pasta, toss quickly, garnish with the minced parsley and basil leaves, and serve immediately.

Serves 4.

RISTORANTE ITALIA
2631 N. Harlem
Chicago, Illinois 60635
(312) 889-5008

Pasta Farfalle alla Pazza

(Butterfly Pasta with Pancetta, Spinach, and Cream)

2 tablespoons unsalted butter
¼ pound pancetta*
½ pound fresh spinach, washed,
    stemmed, and chopped
1 quart heavy cream
Salt
Freshly ground black pepper
1 pound farfalle pasta
3 egg yolks, lightly beaten
¼ cup grated imported Parmesan
    cheese, or to taste

Melt the butter in a skillet. Add the pancetta and fry until crisp. Add
the chopped spinach and sauté for 1 minute. Slowly add the cream
while stirring gently. Add salt and pepper to taste. Cook the sauce for
a few minutes until lightly thickened.

Cook the farfalle in a large pot of boiling, salted water until *al dente.*
Drain.

Carefully toss the farfalle with the sauce. Add the egg yolks and
Parmesan cheese and toss again gently. Serve immediately.

Serves 6.

*Available at Italian grocery stores.

LA STRADA
155 N. Michigan
Chicago, Illinois 60601
(312) 565-2200

Crudaiola   *(Mostaccioli with Salted Ricotta)*

4 tablespoons olive oil
1 medium yellow onion, minced
4 cloves garlic, minced (reserve
   1 teaspoon)
1 pound canned Italian plum
   tomatoes, ground
3 tablespoons salted
   ricotta cheese*

3 tablespoons freshly grated
   Romano cheese
8 to 10 large fresh basil leaves,
   chopped (reserve one
   tablespoon for garnish)
1 pound mostaccioli

Heat the olive oil in a frying pan over low heat. Briefly sauté the onion and garlic. Add the tomatoes, cheeses, and basil. Sauté briefly for 2 to 3 minutes.

Cook the mostaccioli in a large pot of boiling, salted water until *al dente*. Drain well. Place the mostaccioli on a warm platter. Pour the sauce over the pasta, and garnish with the reserved garlic and basil.

Serves 4 to 6.

*Available at Italian grocery stores. Note: Salted ricotta is not the cottage cheese-style ricotta found in supermarkets. It is a hard cheese that should be freshly grated.

RISTORANTE ITALIA
2631 N. Harlem
Chicago, Illinois 60635
(312) 889-5008

Maltagliati con Broccoli
(Mostaccioli with Broccoli and Garlic)

Baking soda
3 to 4 cups fresh broccoli florets
Salt
½ pound mostaccioli
¼ cup virgin olive oil
4 cloves garlic
Freshly ground pepper
2 tablespoons grated imported
    Parmesan cheese

Add a pinch of baking soda to a pot of boiling water. Add the broccoli and cook 4 to 5 minutes. Drain the broccoli and let it cool to room temperature. When the broccoli is cool, chop it into small pieces. Set aside.

In a large pot of boiling, salted water, cook the mostaccioli for 8 to 10 minutes or until *al dente*.

While the mostaccioli is cooking, heat the oil in a large skillet over medium heat. Add the garlic and cook until lightly browned. Discard the garlic. Then add the chopped broccoli to the pan. Sauté over medium heat for 3 minutes. Add salt and pepper to taste.

To serve, drain the mostaccioli and add to the skillet with broccoli. Toss for 30 seconds over medium high heat. Top with the Parmesan cheese and serve immediately.

Serves 4.

LA STRADA
155 N. Michigan Avenue
Chicago, Illinois 60601
(312) 565-2200

Mostaccioli with Arrabbiata Sauce

3 tablespoons olive oil
2 tablespoons minced fresh garlic
½ cup diced yellow onions
1 to 3 teaspoons red pepper
    flakes, to taste
8 ounces hot capicolla, sliced
    julienne
1½ quarts tomato sauce,
    preferably homemade
3 tablespoons minced
    Italian parsley
1½ pounds mostaccioli

Heat the olive oil over medium heat in a saucepan. Sauté the garlic, onions, red pepper flakes, and capicolla until the onions are translucent. Add the tomato sauce and the parsley. Simmer for 10 to 15 minutes. Keep warm.

In a large pot of boiling, salted water, cook the mostaccioli until *al dente*. Drain well. Place the mostaccioli in a large, warm pasta bowl. Add the sauce, toss briefly but thoroughly, and serve immediately.

Serves 4 to 6.

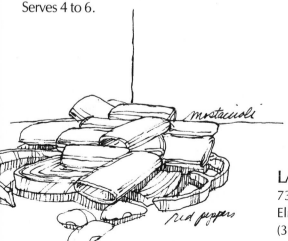

mostaccioli

red peppers

LA CAPANNINA
7353 W. Grand Avenue
Elmwood Park, Illinois 60635
(312) 452-0900

Aushak   (Afghan Ravioli with Leeks)

For the pasta:
2¼ cups all-purpose flour
3 eggs
1 tablespoon olive oil
1 tablespoon water
4 leeks, washed and
    finely chopped
½ teaspoon black pepper
¾ teaspoon salt
Cayenne pepper
3 tablespoons olive oil
1 egg yolk
3 tablespoons water

For the yogurt topping:
3 cups plain yogurt
½ tablespoon garlic powder
½ tablespoon salt

For the meat topping:
3 tablespoons vegetable oil
2 large onions, diced
1 pound ground beef
1 teaspoon salt
1 teaspoon garlic powder
1 teaspoon black pepper
1 teaspoon ground coriander
¼ teaspoon red pepper flakes
¼ teaspoon turmeric
1½ cups tomato sauce

Dry mint, for garnish
Hot red pepper, for garnish

To prepare the pasta:
Combine the flour, eggs, and olive oil in the bowl of a food processor
fitted with a steel blade. Process until the dough forms a ball, adding a
little water if necessary. Wrap the dough tightly in plastic wrap and let it
rest for ½ hour.

To prepare the ravioli:
Roll out the pasta dough in a pasta machine. Cut the dough into 4-inch
squares. In a large bowl, mix and mash the leeks, black pepper, salt,
a dash of cayenne pepper, and olive oil. In a separate bowl, mix the egg
yolk and water. Paint the 4 edges of a ravioli square with the egg and
water mixture. Squeeze the leek mixture to remove excess water and put
1½ tablespoons of the mixture onto each ravioli. Fold the ravoli into a
triangle and tightly seal the edges together. You should have 12 ravioli.
Refrigerate the ravioli until you are ready to cook them.

To prepare the yogurt topping:
Mix the 3 cups of plain yogurt with the garlic powder and salt.

To prepare the meat topping:
Heat the oil in a skillet over medium heat. Sauté the onions until translucent. Add the ground beef and brown. Add the salt, garlic powder, and black pepper. Then add the coriander, red pepper, and turmeric. Add the tomato sauce, stir well, and heat through.

Cook the ravioli in a large pot of boiling water until tender, about 4 to 5 minutes. Drain carefully.

Place ½ cup of yogurt on each of 4 plates. Place 3 ravioli triangles on the yogurt and 1 teaspoon of yogurt on each ravioli. Cover with the ground beef sauce. Sprinkle with dry mint and hot red pepper, if desired.

Serves 4.

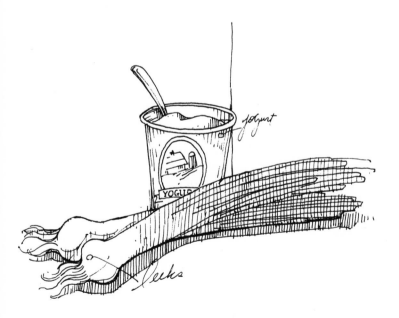

THE HELMAND
3201 N. Halsted
Chicago, Illinois 60657
(312) 935-2447

Squash-Stuffed Ravioli with Prosciutto, Walnuts, and Sage

For the pasta:
2 ¼ cups all-purpose flour
3 eggs
1 tablespoon olive oil
Salt
1 tablespoon water

For the filling:
1 butternut squash,
    about 1 ½ pounds
1 tablespoon olive oil
1 teaspoon chopped garlic
½ cup chicken stock
1 cup drained ricotta cheese

¼ cup grated imported
    Parmesan cheese
1 to 2 eggs
Salt
Pepper
Nutmeg

For the sauce:
2 sticks unsalted butter
½ pound thinly sliced prosciutto,
    cut into julienne strips
½ cup roughly chopped
    toasted walnuts
¼ cup chopped fresh sage leaves

To prepare the pasta:
Put the flour, eggs, olive oil, and a pinch of salt into the bowl of a food processor fitted with a steel blade. Process until the dough forms a ball, adding a little water if necessary. Wrap the dough tightly in plastic wrap, and let rest for ½ hour.

To prepare the filling:
Peel and cube the squash. Sauté the cubes in the olive oil and garlic, adding a little chicken stock from time to time to prevent dryness. When the squash is soft, purée in a food processor. Combine the squash with the ricotta, Parmesan, and 1 egg. If necessary, add a second egg to lighten the mixture to a fluffy consistency. Season with salt, pepper, and a pinch of nutmeg.

To assemble the ravioli:
Roll out the dough in a pasta machine. Pipe the squash filling onto the bottom half of a sheet of pasta, allowing 2 inches of space between each dollop of filling. Dampen the edges of the dough, and fold over the top part of the dough, sealing all around. Press the dough down between the ravioli. Cut the ravioli with a fluted pastry wheel.

To make the sauce:
Melt the butter in a skillet over medium heat and cook until the butter turns a nutty brown, about 10 minutes. Add the prosciutto, walnuts, and sage, and stir.

To finish the dish:
Cook the ravioli in a large pot of boiling, salted water until they rise to the top, about 6 to 8 minutes. Place the ravioli on individual heated serving plates and spoon the sauce over.

Serves 4 to 6.

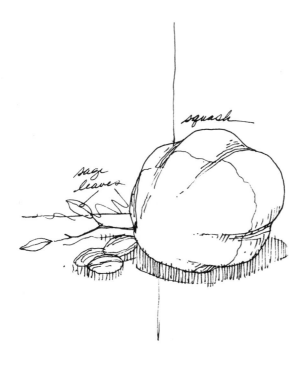

AVANZARE
161 E. Huron
Chicago, Illinois 60611
(312) 337-8056

Spaghetti with Meat Sauce

2 tablespoons olive oil
2 cloves garlic, crushed
1½ pounds sirloin, ground
1 can (1 pound 15 ounces) whole,
    peeled tomatoes
2 cans tomato purée (1 pound
    15 ounces each)
¾ teaspoon sugar
2 tablespoons sweet basil
1 teaspoon Italian seasoning
Salt
Black pepper
1½ pounds spaghetti
Parmesan or Romano cheese,
    freshly grated

Heat the oil in a large skillet and sauté the crushed garlic over medium heat for 2 to 3 minutes. Add the ground sirloin and sauté until the meat loses its pink color. Add the tomatoes, tomato purée, sugar, herbs, and salt and pepper to taste. Bring the sauce to a boil and then lower the heat and simmer for 2 to 3 hours. When the sauce is done, cook the spaghetti in a large pot of boiling, salted water until *al dente*. Pour the sauce over the spaghetti and serve with Parmesan or Romano cheese.

Serves 6 to 10.

LEONA'S
3215 N. Sheffield
Chicago, Illinois 60657
(312) 327-8861

Pasta Primavera

1/4 cup pine nuts
12 cherry tomatoes, halved
4 tablespoons olive oil, divided
4 tablespoons chopped parsley
6 to 8 basil leaves, chopped
Salt
Freshly ground black pepper
1 pound spaghetti
2/3 cup sliced zucchini
2/3 cup broccoli florets
2/3 cup sliced fresh mushrooms
1/4 cup frozen peas

2/3 cup snow peas
6 spears jumbo asparagus, cut in
    1-inch pieces (optional)
3 cloves garlic, chopped

For the sauce:
1/2 stick unsalted butter
1 1/4 cups half-and-half
Salt
Freshly ground black pepper
2 cups grated imported
    Parmesan cheese

Toast the pine nuts in a dry frying pan over medium heat until lightly browned, and set aside.

Marinate the cherry tomatoes for 1 hour in 2 tablespoons of the olive oil, 2 tablespoons of the parsley, 3 to 4 chopped basil leaves, and salt and pepper to taste.

Cook the spaghetti in a large pot of boiling, salted water until *al dente*. Drain.

As the spaghetti finishes cooking, sauté the vegetables in 2 tablespoons of the olive oil, 2 tablespoons of parsley, 3 to 4 chopped basil leaves, and the garlic for about 3 minutes until crisp-tender. Add the pine nuts to the cooked vegetables.

In a small sauce pan, simmer together the butter, half-and-half, and salt and pepper to taste. Add the Parmesan cheese. Toss the drained pasta with the vegetables. Pour the sauce over the vegetables and pasta. Garnish with the marinated tomatoes on top and serve immediately.

Serves 6.

ARNIE'S
1030 N. State Street
Chicago, Illinois 60610
(312) 266-4800

Spaghettini Arrabbiata

2 cloves garlic, chopped
¼ cup extra virgin olive oil
1 each small green, red, and
    yellow bell peppers, cored,
    seeded, and sliced into
    thin strips
1½ pounds eggplant, cubed
1 teaspoon red pepper flakes
1 pound spaghettini
2 ounces imported Parmesan
    cheese, freshly grated
Fresh basil leaves

Sauté the garlic in the olive oil for a minute or two. Add the peppers, eggplant, and red pepper flakes and simmer for 15 minutes. When the sauce is finished, cook the spaghettini in a large pot of boiling, salted water until *al dente*, about 7 to 10 minutes. Drain the spaghettini and top with sauce, Parmesan cheese, and basil.

DA NICOLA
3114 N. Lincoln
Chicago, Illinois 60657
(312) 935-8000

Tortellini alla Panna

1 pound meat-filled tortellini
4 tablespoons unsalted butter
4 leaves fresh sage (If fresh sage is
    unavailable, use ½ teaspoon
    dried, crumbled sage leaves.
    Do not use ground sage.)
1 cup heavy cream
4 tablespoons freshly grated
    imported Parmesan cheese
Nutmeg
Freshly ground black pepper

Cook the tortellini as directed on the package. Drain. Melt the butter
in a large saucepan. Stir in the sage and cook for a few minutes over
medium low heat. Add the drained tortellini and stir. Add the cream, and
stir again. Then add the cheese, a pinch of nutmeg, and pepper to taste.
Stir until the mixture reaches a boil. Serve immediately on warm, deep
plates or in warm pasta bowls with extra cheese on the side.

Serves 4.

BRUNA'S RISTORANTE
2424 S. Oakley
Chicago, Illinois 60608
(312) 254-5550

Thai Fried Rice

5 tablespoons vegetable oil
2 eggs, beaten
1 teaspoon chopped garlic
1 cup diced pork, ham, beef,
    or shrimp
1 cup sliced white onion
5 cups cold cooked white rice
3 to 4 tablespoons fish sauce*
1 tablespoon sugar
½ teaspoon white pepper
2 tablespoons tomato paste
3 green onions, minced

Heat 2 tablespoons of the oil in a wok. Add the beaten eggs, and cook until firm. Remove from the wok, and cut into strips.

Heat 3 tablespoons of the oil over high heat and briefly sauté the garlic. Add the pork, ham, beef, or shrimp and the white onion. Stir-fry briefly until the meat or shrimp is just done. Do not overcook. Add the rice, fish sauce, sugar, white pepper, and tomato paste. Add the egg strips to the rice mixture. Stir constantly for 3 to 4 minutes until everything blends well. Add the green onions and cook for 1 minute longer. Serve immediately.

Serves 6 to 8.

*Available at Oriental grocery stores.

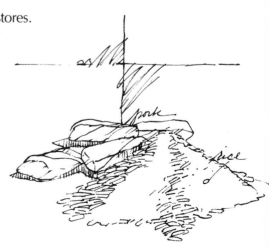

RIVER KWAI
440 N. State Street
Chicago, Illinois 60610
(312) 644-1144

Pad Thai *(Thai Rice Stick)*

½ pound rice noodles*
¾ cup vegetable oil
½ tablespoon minced garlic
2 eggs, beaten
¼ pound small fresh shrimp,
     peeled and deveined
3 tablespoons ground peanuts
2 tablespoons sugar
2 tablespoons chopped
     brine-cured radishes*

4 tablespoons nampla
     (fish sauce)*
3 tablespoons vinegar
½ teaspoon ground red chili
2 cups fresh bean sprouts,
     thoroughly rinsed
Sliced fresh cabbage,
     for garnish
Lime wedges, for garnish

Soak the rice noodles in warm water for 10 minutes. Drain thoroughly. Heat the oil in a large frying pan or wok. Add the garlic and cook for 1 to 2 minutes. Add the noodles, eggs, and shrimp. Toss well and cook for 4 to 5 minutes. Add the peanuts, sugar, radishes, fish sauce, vinegar, red chili, and bean sprouts. Stir very thoroughly. Serve with the cabbage slices and lime wedges for garnish.

Serves 4 to 6.

*Available at Oriental grocery stores.

SIAM CAFÉ
4712 N. Sheridan
Chicago, Illinois 60640
(312) 769-6602

Crispy Rice Crust

For the sauce:
Vegetable oil
1 teaspoon minced garlic
1 teaspoon minced ginger
¼ pound ground pork
1 teaspoon salt
1 teaspoon sugar
½ teaspoon soy sauce
½ cup ground peanuts
¼ cup sesame seeds
1 cup water
Chili oil, to taste*

½ teaspoon egg-shade food color
1 teaspoon salt
4 to 6 scallions, sliced lengthwise
1 medium onion, thinly sliced
1 pound fresh bean sprouts
Lettuce, for garnish
Cucumber slices, for garnish
Cilantro or mint, for garnish

For the rice crust:
Vegetable oil
1 cup lean pork, cut into strips
8 to 12 large shrimp, peeled
    and deveined
½ pound rice flour*
1½ cups cold water
2 eggs, lightly beaten

To prepare the sauce:
Heat 1 tablespoon of the vegetable oil in a skillet or wok. Add the garlic and ginger. Add the ground pork and stir-fry until brown. Add the salt, sugar, soy sauce, peanuts, sesame seeds, water, and chili oil. Stir and simmer for 15 minutes.

To prepare the rice crusts:
Heat 1 tablespoon of the vegetable oil in a non-stick skillet. Stir-fry the pork until it is white. Add the shrimp and stir-fry quickly.

Mix the rice flour in a bowl with the cold water. Add the eggs, food color, and salt and stir until well blended. In a separate 6-to 8-inch non-stick skillet, heat 1 to 2 tablespoons of the vegetable oil. Pour a ladleful (about ½ cup) of the rice batter into the skillet. Turn the skillet to spread the batter. Add 2 cooked shrimp and about one quarter of the pork strips.

Cover the skillet and lower the heat. Cook for 3 minutes. Remove the cover and top with some scallions, onion, and bean sprouts. Cover and cook another 2 minutes or until the bottom of the pancake is crispy and brown. Remove from the pan and fold the rice crust like a taco. Repeat until all the batter has been used. When the rice crusts finish cooking, keep them warm.

Arrange each rice crust on a plate garnished with the lettuce, cucumbers, and the cilantro or mint. Serve the sauce with the rice crusts.

Serves 4 to 6.

*Available at Oriental grocery stores.

HUÉ
1138 W. Argyle
Chicago, Illinois 60640
(312) 275-4044

Singapore Rice Noodle

½ pound rice noodles*
Corn oil
1 medium green bell pepper,
*   sliced julienne*
1 medium onion, halved and
*   thinly sliced*
¼ teaspoon salt
1 tablespoon water

¾ pound bean sprouts
¼ pound barbecued pork,
*   sliced julienne**
1 egg, fried and sliced into
*   thin strips*
½ teaspoon sesame oil
½ teaspoon dry sherry
½ tablespoon curry powder

Parboil the noodles for 4 to 5 minutes. Drain and place in a warm bowl. Cover with a towel for 5 minutes or until the noodles soften.

Heat ½ tablespoon of corn oil in a wok. Stir-fry the green pepper and onion for 1 minute. Add the salt and the water. Cover and cook for 1 minute. Remove and set aside. Add ½ tablespoon of corn oil to the wok and stir-fry the bean sprouts for 30 seconds. Remove and set aside. Add another ½ tablespoon of corn oil to the wok and stir-fry the barbecued pork and the eggs. Remove and set aside. Add another ½ tablespoon of corn oil to the wok and stir-fry the barbecued pork and the eggs. Remove and set aside.

Add 1 tablespoon of corn oil, the sesame oil, sherry, and curry powder to the wok. Add the vegetable-egg-barbecued pork mixture and stir-fry for 1 minute. Add the noodles. Mix well, cook for 2 minutes, and serve immediately.

Serves 4.

*Available at Oriental grocery stores.

HONG MIN
221 W. Cermak Road
Chicago, Illinois 60616
(312) 842-5026

Oscar's Noodles

1 pound whole wheat spaghetti
2 teaspoons salt
2 teaspoons vegetable oil
4 tablespoons sesame oil, divided
1½ tablespoons roasted
    sesame seeds
1 tablespoon chopped fresh garlic
1 tablespoon peeled and minced
    fresh ginger

⅔ cup green bell peppers,
    sliced julienne
⅔ cup grated carrots
⅔ cup steamed and finely
    chopped broccoli florets
2 tablespoons water
2 to 3 tablespoons tamari
    soy sauce
4 green onions, chopped

Add the spaghetti to a large pot of boiling water to which you have added the salt and the vegetable oil. Cook until *al dente*. Rinse the cooked spaghetti in hot water and drain. While still hot, toss the spaghetti with 2 tablespoons of the sesame oil and the roasted sesame seeds. Set aside.

Heat the 2 remaining tablespoons of sesame oil in a large sauté pan. Add the garlic and ginger. Sauté lightly over medium heat. Add the peppers, carrots, broccoli, and 2 tablespoons of water. Sauté for 1 minute. Add the vegetable mixture to the pasta. Season with the tamari soy sauce. Garnish with the green onions.

Serves 4.

THE BREAD SHOP
3400 N. Halsted
Chicago, Illinois 60657
(312) 528-8108

Vegetarian

Huevos Las Mañanitas (Eggs with Avocado)

2 quarts water
1 cup white vinegar
8 eggs
2 cups tomato sauce
Salsa (optional)
4 ripe avocados, peeled and
    halved
8 slices Chihuahua cheese (Swiss
    cheese may be substituted)*

Preheat the oven to 350°.

Pour the water and the vinegar into a large pot and bring to a boil. Crack open the eggs and gently slip them into the boiling water. Poach the eggs until set. Heat the tomato sauce in a saucepan. Add salsa to taste, if desired.

Arrange the avocado halves in a baking dish. Place one egg on each half. Pour some hot tomato sauce over each egg and top with a cheese slice. Bake approximately 5 to 10 minutes until cheese melts. Serve with refried beans and corn tortillas if desired.

Serves 4.

*Chihuahua cheese is available at Mexican grocery stores.

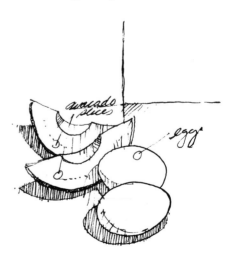

LAS MAÑANITAS
3523 N. Halsted
Chicago, Illinois 60657
(312) 528-2109

Golden Leek Frittata

2 tablespoons unsalted butter
2 large leeks (white part only),
    well rinsed and thinly sliced
3 eggs, beaten
3 tablespoons freshly grated
    imported Parmesan cheese
5 tablespoons grated
    Mozzarella cheese
Salt
Pepper
Italian black olives, for garnish
Tomato slices, for garnish
Fresh tomato sauce (optional)

Preheat the broiler.

Melt the butter over medium heat in an omelette pan and sauté the sliced leeks until golden. Add the cheeses to the beaten eggs. Pour the egg-cheese mixture onto the sautéed leeks and cook until the bottom is set. Place the omelette pan under the broiler for a moment or two until the top of the frittata is cooked. Salt and pepper to taste. Place the frittata on a serving dish and garnish with the olives and tomatoes. If desired, serve with a simple fresh tomato sauce.

Serves 4 as an appetizer or 2 as an entrée.

DA NICOLA
3114 N. Lincoln Avenue
Chicago, Illinois 60657
(312) 935-8000

Broccoli Vegetable Pancakes with Four-Cheese Sauce

For the four-cheese sauce:
1 pound ricotta cheese
½ pound cottage cheese
⅛ pound feta cheese
¼ pound Montrechet goat cheese
1 cup olive oil or vegetable oil
½ teaspoon salt
¼ teaspoon cumin
1 teaspoon turmeric
3 large jalapeño peppers or
  to taste
⅛ teaspoon freshly ground
  black pepper
½ cup evaporated milk

½ teaspoon freshly ground
  black pepper
1 teaspoon coarse (Kosher) salt
1 tablespoon baking powder
1 pound all-purpose flour
1 tablespoon minced parsley
32 ounces vegetable oil
Black olives, for garnish
Hard-boiled egg wedges,
  for garnish

For the broccoli pancakes:
2 pounds fresh broccoli florets
5 cloves garlic, crushed
1 pound Spanish onions, minced
8 eggs, beaten

To prepare the cheese sauce:
Combine the 4 cheeses with the olive oil, salt, cumin, turmeric, jalapeños, and black pepper in a food processor or blender. Process using on-off turns, scraping down the sides of the container as necessary, until the mixture is creamy and smooth. With the motor running, add enough milk to thin the sauce to the desired consistency. Heat the sauce gently over low heat, stirring frequently.

To prepare the broccoli pancakes:
Steam the broccoli for about 10 minutes until just tender. Set it aside to cool. Combine the garlic and onions in a large bowl. Chop the broccoli into ½-inch pieces and add to the bowl. Add the eggs. Then add the spices and remaining ingredients, except the vegetable oil. Mix well.

Heat the oil in a deep skillet until hot but not smoking. Coat an ice cream scoop by dipping it into the hot oil. Fill the scoop with batter, put the batter in the hot oil, and fry until crisp and golden. Drain on paper towels. Serve hot with the warm cheese sauce. If you wish, serve on a bed of lettuce and parsley, and garnish with black olives and wedges of hard-boiled egg.

Serves 6 to 8.

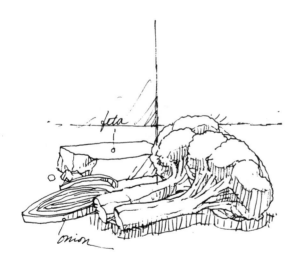

LA LLAMA
3811 N. Ashland Avenue
Chicago, Illinois 60613
(312) 327-7756

Eggplant Parmesan

3 pounds eggplant
2 eggs
2 tablespoons milk
1/4 cup water
2 cups whole wheat pastry flour
1 1/2 teaspoons salt
1 1/2 teaspoons oregano

1 1/2 teaspoons garlic powder
Olive oil
4 cups tomato sauce
1 pound mozzarella cheese,
    grated
1/2 cup freshly grated imported
    Parmesan cheese

Cut the eggplant into 1/4-inch slices. Soak in salted water for at least 30 minutes. Drain.

Preheat the oven to 350°.

In one bowl, mix the eggs, milk, and water until well blended. In a second bowl, mix the whole wheat pastry flour, salt, oregano, and garlic powder. Dip the eggplant slices into the egg mixture first and then into the flour mixture. Place the slices on 2 oiled baking trays. Bake for 15 minutes, turning once.

Oil a large casserole with olive oil. Layer the casserole as follows: 1 cup tomato sauce, half of the eggplant, half of the mozzarella cheese, 1 cup of tomato sauce, the remaining eggplant, the remaining mozzarella cheese, the remaining tomato sauce, and all the Parmesan cheese. Bake in a 350° oven for 30 minutes or until the casserole is heated through and the eggplant is tender.

Serves 6 to 8.

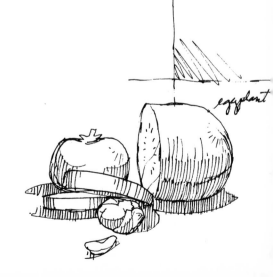

THE BREAD SHOP
3400 N. Halsted
Chicago, Illinois 60657
(312) 528-8108

Candied Sweet Potatoes

6 medium-sized sweet potatoes
¾ cup brown sugar
¾ cup white sugar
1½ tablespoons freshly squeezed
        lemon juice (optional)
4 ounces (1 stick) butter or
        margarine
Nutmeg
Salt
2 to 3 cups water

Preheat the oven to 350°.

Place the sweet potatoes in a medium-sized pot. Add water to cover. Boil the potatoes until they are nearly tender. Do not overcook. Cool the potatoes immediately under cold water. Peel the potatoes, and cut them lengthwise into ¾-inch slices or 2-inch squares. Place the potatoes in a shallow baking dish.

In a large pot, mix all of the remaining ingredients and bring to a boil. Keep boiling until the mixture becomes slightly thick. Stir constantly. Pour the mixture over the potatoes.

Bake for approximately 45 minutes or until the potatoes are glazed.

Serves 4 to 6.

ARMY & LOU'S
420-22 E. 78th Street
Chicago, Illinois 60619
(312) 483-6550

Vegetarian Chili

6 cups canned kidney beans,
    drained and rinsed
1 large can (28 ounces) whole
    tomatoes, crushed
1 can (15 ounces) tomato purée
¼ cup chili powder or to taste
1 tablespoon cumin or to taste
1 tablespoon dry mustard
1 tablespoon garlic powder
1½ teaspoons cayenne pepper
    or to taste
1 tablespoon honey

2 tablespoons tamari soy sauce
1 medium onion, diced
1 medium green bell pepper,
    cored, seeded, and diced
¼ pound mushrooms, cleaned
    and sliced
Grated cheddar cheese,
    for garnish
Green onion, chopped,
    for garnish

Add all but the last 2 ingredients to a large stock pot. Mix well.
Bring the mixture to a boil over medium-high heat. Reduce heat and
simmer until the vegetables are tender, about 2 hours. Ladle into soup
bowls and garnish with the grated cheddar cheese and green onion.
Serve with corn bread.

Serves 6 to 8.

HEARTLAND CAFÉ
7000 N. Glenwood
Chicago, Illinois 60626
(312) 465-8005

Lentil Burgers

1 cup water
¼ cup lentils
¼ cup uncooked brown rice
½ white onion, diced
½ cup crumbled cornbread
2 tablespoons tomato sauce or
    Mexican salsa
2 tablespoons tamari soy sauce
¼ teaspoon celery seed
1 teaspoon garlic powder
2 tablespoons corn oil

Pour the water, lentils, and rice into a large pot. Cook over low heat for 45 minutes. Transfer the lentils and rice to a bowl. Add the onion and cornbread and mash together. Mix in the remaining ingredients except the corn oil. When the mixture is cool enough to handle, form into 4 patties. Sauté the lentil burgers in corn oil until golden brown. Serve in pita bread or on hamburger buns with cheese and the condiments of your choice.

Serves 4.

HEARTLAND CAFÉ
7000 N. Glenwood
Chicago, Illinois 60626
(312) 465-8005

Baked Filled Acorn Squash

4 acorn squash
4 tablespoons unsalted butter,
 melted
Nutmeg
Cinnamon
Thyme
Salt
1¾ cups water
1 cup brown rice or white
 basmati rice
1 tablespoon vegetable oil
1 small yellow onion, diced
1 stalk celery, diced
1 medium baking apple, diced
Sage
Freshly ground black pepper

2 cups apple cider
¾ cup mirin (non-alcoholic
 rice wine)*
2 tablespoons tamari soy sauce*
3 tablespoons arrowroot with
 enough water added to
 make a thin paste

To prepare the squash:
Preheat the oven to 350°.

Cut the squash in half lengthwise through the stems. Scoop out the seeds and set the squash in a baking dish. Fill the dish with ½ inch of water. Season the squash with melted butter on each and a dash of nutmeg, cinnamon, thyme, and salt. Bake, covered, for 30 to 45 minutes or until tender.

In a medium-sized pot, bring the water to a boil. Wash the rice and add it to the boiling water. Reduce the heat and cook covered for 10 to 15 minutes.

Heat the vegetable oil in a saucepan. Sauté the onion, celery, and apple until the onion is translucent. Season with sage, thyme, salt, and pepper to taste. Add the sautéed vegetables to the rice and mix together.

Remove the squash from the oven. Using an ice-cream scoop, fill each squash cavity with the rice-apple mixture.

To prepare the apple-mirin glaze:
Mix the cider, mirin, and tamari soy sauce in a small saucepan over high

heat. Whisk in the arrowroot paste. If necessary, thin the glaze with a little water to the consistency of a light syrup.

Place the baked squash on serving plates and top each with the glaze. Serve immediately.

Note: You may want to add one or more of the following to the squash filling: green peas, toasted walnuts, and raisins.

Serves 4.

*Available at health food stores.

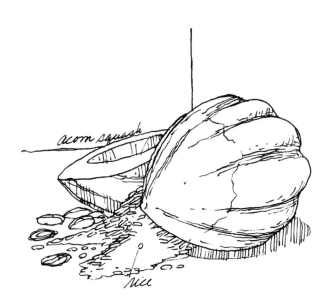

THE CHICAGO DINER
3411 N. Halsted
Chicago, Illinois 60657
(312) 935-6696

Diner's Scrambled Tofu

1 tablespoon sunflower seeds
    or other seeds or nuts
1 tablespoon sesame seeds
1 tablespoon tamari soy sauce
1 tablespoon sesame tahini*
1 tub firm tofu, drained
2 green onions, chopped, or
    an equal amount of other
    vegetables, chopped into
    small pieces

Mix the sunflower seeds, sesame seeds, tamari soy sauce, and sesame tahini in a large bowl. Blend into a paste. Crumble the tofu and add to the seed paste. Blend well with a potato masher or fork. Sauté the mixture in a dry skillet until lightly browned. Add the green onions or assorted vegetables to taste. May be served hot or cold. Serve with corn bread and rice.

Note: For a more highly seasoned dish, add garlic, fresh herbs, or spices to taste.

Serves 2.

*Available at health food stores.

THE CHICAGO DINER
3411 N. Halsted
Chicago, Illinois 60657
(312) 935-6696

Dairy Grinder Sub

For the Dairy Grinder spread
(enough for 6 sandwiches):
½ cup sliced onion
1 cup mayonnaise
⅔ cup sour cream
2 cloves garlic, put through
*   a press*
⅓ cup catsup
Salt
¼ cup sweet pickle relish
Freshly ground pepper to taste

For 1 Dairy Grinder Sub:
French bread, about
*   8 inches long*
2 lettuce leaves (romaine, Boston,
*   or iceberg, for example)*
4 slices jack cheese
2 slices tomato
2 slices red onion
2 slices cucumber, cut lengthwise
4 slices avocado
1 ounce fresh sprouts

To prepare the spread:
Purée the onion in a food processor or blender. In a large bowl,
mix together the remaining ingredients. Add the puréed onions and
blend thoroughly.

To prepare the sandwich:
Cut the French bread in half horizontally. Cover the bottom half with
a layer of the Dairy Grinder Spread. Then layer each of the sandwich
ingredients on top according to the above order. End with a second layer
of lettuce and cheese. Top with the sprouts. Spread the remaining half of
the French bread with the Dairy Grinder spread to complete the sandwich.

Serves 6.

BLIND FAITH CAFÉ
525 Dempster Street
Evanston, Illinois 60201
(312) 328-6875

Desserts

Baked Bananas with Caramel

1 pound sugar
½ cup water
1 cup heavy cream
4 bananas
Sugar
4 ounces pistachios, chopped
Whipped cream (optional)

Preheat the broiler.

Put 1 pound of sugar and the water in a heavy skillet. Dissolve the sugar by shaking the pan. Do not stir. When the sugar has dissolved, place the skillet on low heat. Cook the sugar syrup until it is a light amber color. Remove from heat. Carefully add the cream ¼ cup at a time to the syrup. The syrup will splatter easily. When the bubbles die down, stir with a whisk. Reserve.

Peel the bananas, split them lengthwise, and lay the cut sides down on a broiler pan. Sprinkle with sugar. Place the bananas under the broiler until the sugar carmelizes, about 2 or 3 minutes. Watch carefully. The sugar burns easily.

Place 2 banana halves on each serving plate. Ladle a little caramel sauce over each. Sprinkle with chopped pistachios and top with whipped cream if desired.

Serves 4.

CAFÉ BA-BA-REEBA!
2024 N. Halsted
Chicago, Illinois 60614
(312) 935-5000

Bananas Borrachas

4 small ripe bananas
2 tablespoons butter
4 tablespoons piloncillo
    (Mexican brown sugar)*
1 ounce banana liqueur
½ teaspoon cinnamon
½ ounce rum
4 scoops best-quality vanilla
    ice cream

Peel and slice each banana in half lengthwise. Melt the butter in a large skillet on low heat. Add the brown sugar. Stir constantly until the sugar dissolves. Add the banana liqueur and stir. Place the bananas in the skillet and simmer for about 2 minutes on each side. Dust with the cinnamon. Add the rum and light with a match. Allow the alcohol to burn off. Place a scoop of ice cream on each of 4 dessert plates. Place 2 banana halves around each scoop of ice cream and pour the sauce over all. Serve immediately.

Serves 4.

*Available at Mexican grocery stores. Regular brown sugar may be substituted, but the taste will be altered.

LAS MAÑANITAS
3523 N. Halsted
Chicago, Illinois 60657
(312) 528-2109

Caramel Apples with Rum and Ice Cream

6 small or 4 large baking apples
Juice of ½ lemon
12 tablespoons (1½ sticks)
        unsalted butter
1⅓ cups sugar
1 teaspoon fresh lemon juice
1½ tablespoons dark rum
12 scoops coffee ice cream

Peel, core, and cut the apples into ¼-inch slices. To prevent the apple slices from turning brown, place the slices in a bowl of water to which you have added the juice of half a lemon.

Melt the butter in a skillet over medium heat. When the butter has melted, stir in the sugar and the teaspoon of lemon juice. Cook over medium heat until the mixture turns a light brown caramel. Drain the apple slices and pat dry. Add the slices to the caramel and cook for 2 to 3 minutes. Stir in the rum and remove from heat. Place 2 scoops of coffee ice cream in each of 6 dessert bowls. Spoon the caramel mixture over the ice cream and serve immediately.

Serves 6.

JIMMY'S PLACE
3420 N. Elston Avenue
Chicago, Illinois 60618
(312) 539-2999

Cherry Clafoutis

For the cherry marinade:
1 pound of very ripe bing
  cherries, pitted
½ cup Kirsch
1 tablespoon sugar

For the pastry:
1 cup flour
2 tablespoons sugar
¼ teaspoon salt
6 tablespoons unsalted butter
1 egg yolk

½ teaspoon vanilla
1 tablespoon fresh lemon juice

For the filling:
4 eggs, well beaten
1 cup whipping cream
½ cup sugar
1 teaspoon vanilla
2 tablespoons cake flour
2 tablespoons Kirsch
  (or more to taste)

To marinate the cherries:
Put the cherries into a large bowl. Add the Kirsch and sugar.
Let the cherries marinate for 2 hours, stirring occasionally.

To prepare the pastry:
Mix the flour with the sugar and the salt in a large bowl. Cut in the butter
with a pastry blender until the mixture resembles coarse crumbs. Make a
well in the center of the flour. Add the egg yolk, vanilla, and lemon juice.
Mix with a fork just until dough gathers into a ball. Cover in plastic wrap
and refrigerate for 30 minutes. Roll out the dough on a lightly floured
surface to ⅛-inch thickness. Fit into a 10-inch tart pan with a removable
bottom. Refrigerate for 5 minutes. Preheat the oven to 325°.

To prepare the filling:
Thoroughly mix the 4 eggs, whipping cream, sugar, vanilla, cake flour,
and Kirsch. Drain the cherries. Remove the tart pan from the refrigerator.
Arrange the cherries carefully on the dough. Spoon the egg-cream
mixture over the cherries. Bake for 40 to 45 minutes until a knife inserted
1 inch from the edge is withdrawn clean. Do not overbake. Cool on a
wire rack. Serve warm.

Serves 8.

LE FRANÇAIS
269 S. Milwaukee
Wheeling, Illinois 60090
(312) 541-7470

Poached Pears with Port Wine Glaze

For the poaching liquid:
2½ cups sugar
3 cups water
1 cup dry white wine
1 cinnamon stick
1 clove
Zest (orange part only) and juice
    from 1 orange

5 firm, ripe pears

For the port wine glaze:
½ bottle port
Zest (orange part only) from
    1 orange
1 cinnamon stick
1 large slice fresh ginger
1 clove
1 tablespoon cornstarch
Juice from 1 orange

Combine the ingredients for the poaching liquid in a pot large enough to accommodate all of the pears. Boil the liquid for 15 to 20 minutes over high heat. Peel the pears, leaving their stems on. Reduce the heat to low and poach the pears until knife-tender. Remove the pears from the poaching liquid and allow them to cool slightly.

Combine the first 5 ingredients for the port wine glaze in a saucepan. Bring the mixture to a boil over high heat and reduce by half. When the glaze has been reduced, combine the cornstarch with the fresh orange juice and add to the glaze to thicken it slightly.

To serve, lift each pear by its stem and dip the pear into the glaze, coating it evenly. Place each pear on a serving dish covered with 1 or 2 tablespoons of the glaze.

Serves 5.

PRINTER'S ROW
550 S. Dearborn
Chicago, Illinois 60605
(312) 461-0780

Rhubarb Yogurt Cream

6 ounces low-fat yogurt
13 tablespoons sugar
1 teaspoon vanilla
1 tablespoon rum
5 ounces fresh rhubarb
4 cups water
10 whole black peppercorns
1 clove
¼ vanilla bean
3 sheets of gelatin, softened
      in cold water
¾ cup whipped cream

Whisk the yogurt, 5 tablespoons of the sugar, the vanilla, and rum together in a large bowl.

Clean and dice the rhubarb into large chunks. Bring the water, 8 tablespoons of the sugar, the peppercorns, clove, and vanilla bean to a boil. Strain the peppercorns, clove, and vanilla bean from the water. Add the rhubarb and simmer until it is soft (3 to 5 minutes). Remove the rhubarb from the water and purée in a blender until smooth. Pour the hot purée into a second bowl and gently whisk in the softened gelatin. Add this purée to the yogurt mixture. When the yogurt mixture is cool, fold in the whipped cream until fully incorporated. Spoon into dessert goblets and chill until firm, about 4 to 6 hours. May be served with a caramel or vanilla sauce.

Serves 4.

DIETERLE'S
550 S. McLean Boulevard
Elgin, Illinois 60123
(312) 697-7311

Crème Caramel

4 tablespoons (½ stick)
    unsalted butter
4 eggs
¾ cup sugar
1 teaspoon vanilla extract
1⅓ cups milk
1 cup sugar
¼ cup water
Strawberries, for garnish
Kiwi fruit, for garnish

To prepare the custard:
Preheat the oven to 325°.

Melt the butter in a saucepan over low heat. Beat the eggs for 1 to 2 minutes. To the eggs, add the sugar, vanilla, milk, and melted butter. Mix together and set aside.

To prepare the caramel sauce:
Heat 1 cup of sugar and ¼ cup of water gently, stirring constantly with a long-handled spoon for about 8 to 10 minutes until the sugar is caramelized. Allow sauce to cool for 5 minutes.

Pour the caramel into 4 individual custard cups. Pour the custard on top of the caramel. Place the cups in a baking dish filled with ½ inch of hot water. Bake the custard in this water bath for 25 minutes. The custard is done when a knife inserted near the edge of the cup comes out clean.

Refrigerate for 4 hours. Unmold so that the caramel is on the top. Garnish with sliced strawberries and kiwi fruit, if desired.

Serves 4.

LA BOHÈME
566 Chestnut Street
Winnetka, Illinois 60093
(312) 446-4600

Grape Nut Custard

1 quart milk
1 cup Grape Nuts cereal
1 tablespoon unsalted
      butter, melted
6 eggs, beaten
¾ cup sugar
4 ounces evaporated milk
Pinch of nutmeg
Whipped cream

Preheat the oven to 300°.

Mix all of the above ingredients except the whipped cream in a large mixing bowl. Pour the mixture into a 10 x 12-inch casserole. Place this casserole in a larger pan or casserole half filled with hot water. Bake for 45 minutes. The custard is done when an inserted toothpick comes out clean. Serve warm or cold with whipped cream.

Serves 8 to 10.

ANN SATHER
929 W. Belmont
Chicago, Illinois 60657
(312) 348-2378

Tiramisu   (Whipped Mascarpone with Marsala)

3 egg yolks
⅜ cup sugar
1 egg white
¾ pound mascarpone cheese
1 tablespoon Marsala wine
12 ladyfinger cookies
½ cup brewed, cold espresso
Grated bittersweet chocolate,
*   for garnish*

Whip the egg yolks and sugar together until the mixture thickens and forms a ribbon when the beaters are lifted. Whip the egg white until soft peaks form. Add the cheese to the egg-yolk mixture and mix until smooth and well blended. Add the Marsala and mix. Fold in the beaten egg white.

Dip the ladyfingers in the espresso and stand 2 in each of 6 martini glasses or dessert goblets. Fill with the mascarpone mixture, sprinkle grated chocolate on top, and serve.

Serves 6.

SPIAGGIA
980 N. Michigan Avenue
Chicago, Illinois 60611
(312) 280-2750

Orange Bread Pudding

8 slices of best-quality white bread,
crust removed
1½ cups milk
¼ pound (1 stick) unsalted
butter, softened
1 cup sugar, divided
4 egg yolks

2 tablespoons grated orange zest
(orange part only)
¼ teaspoon nutmeg
¼ teaspoon cinnamon
½ cup raisins
4 egg whites
Bourbon (optional)

Preheat the oven to 375°.

Soak the bread in the milk in a large bowl. In another large bowl, cream together the butter and ½ cup sugar. Add the egg yolks one at a time, mixing well. Fold in the orange zest, nutmeg, cinnamon, and raisins. Fold in the soaked bread.

Beat the egg whites and ½ cup sugar until stiff. Fold the egg whites into the bread mixture.

Butter and sugar a 10x12x2-inch pan. Pour the mixture into the pan. Place the pudding in a water bath and bake for approximately 40 to 50 minutes or until a knife inserted comes out clean. Serve warm, sprinkled with bourbon if you wish.

Serves 8.

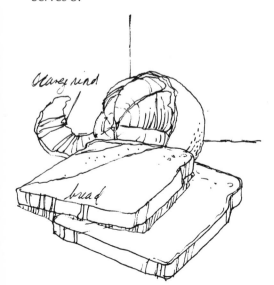

FOLEY'S ON OHIO
211 E. Ohio
Chicago, Illinois 60601
(312) 645-1261

Chocolate Chip Pine Weazel Cookies

½ pound (2 sticks) unsalted butter,
softened
1 cup sugar
½ cup firmly packed brown sugar
¾ teaspoon baking soda
¾ teaspoon salt

1½ teaspoons pure vanilla extract
2 eggs
2 cups flour
1 pound semi-sweet
chocolate chips
2 cups roasted pine nuts

Preheat the oven to 350°.

Cream together the butter, both sugars, baking soda, and salt until blended thoroughly. Add the vanilla, eggs, and flour. Mix until well blended. Mix in the chocolate chips and pine nuts. Drop the dough from a teaspoon onto greased cookie sheets. Bake for about 10 to 15 minutes or until golden.

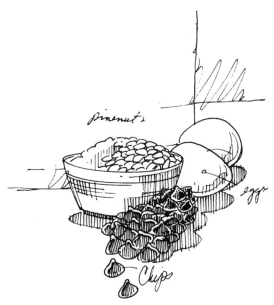

CONVITO ITALIANO
11 E. Chestnut Street
Chicago, Illinois 60611
(312) 943-2984

Chocolate Hazelnut Mousse

7 ounces bittersweet chocolate,
   chopped
3 ounces Frangelica liqueur
1 pint whipping cream
½ cup chopped roasted
   hazelnuts

5 egg whites at room temperature
¼ teaspoon cream of tartar
Salt
½ cup sugar
Whipped cream (optional)

Put the chocolate and the Frangelica in the top of a double boiler. Melt the chocolate slowly until the mixture is smooth. Let cool slightly. While the chocolate is melting, whip the cream to soft peaks in a large, chilled bowl. Fold the cooled chocolate and the hazelnuts into the whipped cream.

Put the egg whites into a clean stainless steel or copper bowl. Beat with an electric mixer at slow speed until the whites begin to foam. Add the cream of tartar and a pinch of salt and continue to beat, increasing the speed to high and adding the sugar gradually. Beat the egg whites until they form soft peaks. Do not let the egg whites become stiff and dry. Fold the egg whites into the chocolate-cream mixture. Spoon the mousse into individual dessert dishes or glasses and chill at least 1 hour before serving. Mousse may be garnished with whipped cream if desired.

Serves 6.

LA CAPANNINA
7353 W. Grand Avenue
Elmwood Park, Illinois 60635
(312) 452-0900

Steve's Hot Apple Cake with Caramel-Pecan Sauce

1½ cups flour
1½ cups white sugar
2 teaspoons baking soda
2 teaspoons baking powder
2 teaspoons cinnamon
1 teaspoon nutmeg
1 teaspoon salt
1 cup vegetable oil
3 eggs

2 cups peeled and finely chopped
    Granny Smith apples
2 cups chopped pecans, divided
2 tablespoons unsalted butter
2 cups whipping cream
2¼ cups dark brown sugar,
    firmly packed
12 scoops vanilla ice cream

Preheat the oven to 375°.

To prepare the cake:
In a large mixing bowl, combine the flour, white sugar, baking soda, baking powder, cinnamon, nutmeg, and salt. Add the vegetable oil and beat with a hand mixer until blended. Add the eggs, one at a time, beating after each addition. Add the apples and 1 cup of the pecans. Bake in a greased 10-inch springform pan for 55 to 60 minutes.

To prepare the caramel-pecan sauce:
Melt the butter in a saucepan over medium heat. Add the remaining 1 cup of pecans and stir until warm. Do not brown. Add the cream and dark brown sugar. Stir and bring to a boil. Continue stirring while the mixture boils for about 6 to 7 minutes. Remove from heat to cool.

Serve the cake warm. Add a scoop of vanilla ice cream and top with the warm caramel-pecan sauce.

Serves 12.

MEDICI
2610 N. Halsted
Chicago, Illinois 60614
(312) 935-7300

Carrot Cake

For the cake:
1½ cups honey
1½ cups melted unsalted butter
1 tablespoon vanilla
Zest (yellow part only)
    of 1 lemon
4 eggs
2 cups whole wheat flour
2 cups pastry flour
1 teaspoon salt
½ teaspoon allspice

½ tablespoon cinnamon
1 tablespoon baking powder
1 pound carrots, grated
¾ cup toasted walnuts
¾ cup raisins

For the icing:
¾ pound cream cheese, softened
½ tablespoon plus 1 teaspoon
    vanilla
½ cup honey

To prepare the cake:
Preheat the oven to 350°.

In a large bowl, mix the honey, melted butter, vanilla, and the lemon zest.
Add the eggs one at a time, and mix well. In a separate bowl, mix the
flours, salt, allspice, cinnamon, and baking powder. Stir in the carrots.
Add to the wet mixture and stir well. Add the walnuts and raisins. Pour
into a 9-inch buttered cake pan. Bake for 45 minutes. Cool.

To prepare the icing:
In a mixing bowl, whip the cream cheese, vanilla, and honey together.
Frost the cooled cake.

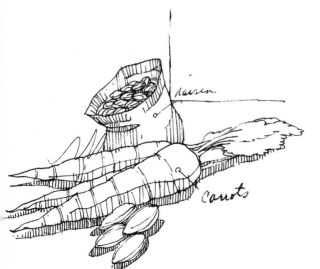

HEARTLAND CAFÉ
7000 N. Glenwood
Chicago, Illinois 60626
(312) 465-8005

Bittersweet Chocolate Raspberry Torte

1¼ pound Ghiradelli bittersweet chocolate, broken into chunks	4 egg whites Salt
6 tablespoons unsalted butter	3 tablespoons black raspberry preserves
¼ cup water	1 pint fresh raspberries
4 egg yolks	Lightly sweetened whipped cream
¼ cup sugar	
1 tablespoon flour	

Butter and flour a 9-inch springform pan. Preheat the oven to 425°.

Combine the chocolate, butter, and water in the top of a double boiler. Melt over simmering water, stirring to blend. Cool until the mixture is just slightly warmer than room temperature.

Combine the egg yolks and sugar in a mixing bowl and beat until the yolks are pale yellow and form a ribbon when the beaters are lifted. Continue beating and pour in the chocolate mixture. Blend well. Mix in the flour.

In a clean mixing bowl, beat the egg whites until they foam. Add a small pinch of salt and continue beating until the whites form soft peaks. Stir ⅓ of the whites into the chocolate mixture to lighten it. Then pour the chocolate mixture over the remaining whites and fold in quickly but gently. Pour this batter into the prepared pan and bake for 15 minutes only. Let the cake sit overnight, covered. The cake will sink in the middle.

Release the cake from the pan. Melt the preserves and spread them over the sunken part of the cake. Arrange the raspberries over the top of the cake. Serve with lightly sweetened whipped cream.

Serves 10.

LESLEE'S
Sherman at Grove
Evanston, Illinois 60201
(312) 328-8304

Chocolate Banana Cheesecake

1½ cups crumbled graham crackers
1¼ cups sugar
2 teaspoons cinnamon
4 tablespoons unsalted
    butter, melted
32 ounces cream cheese,
    at room temperature

4 large eggs
1 cup cream
2 ripe bananas, peeled
Pure vanilla extract to taste
½ cup banana liqueur
12 ounces semi-sweet chocolate

Preheat the oven to 325°.

To prepare the crust:
Mix the graham cracker crumbs with ¼ cup of the sugar and the
cinnamon. Then add the melted butter. Press the crust mixture onto
the bottom and sides of a 9-inch springform pan and surround the pan
with double aluminum foil.

To prepare the filling:
With a mixer, blend the cream cheese with the remaining sugar, the eggs,
cream, bananas, vanilla, and banana liqueur. Pour the mixture into
the crust. Melt the chocolate in a double boiler and swirl on top of the
cheese mixture.

Bake for 2 hours. Turn the oven off. Cool the cheesecake in the oven for
half an hour. Serve chilled or at room temperature.

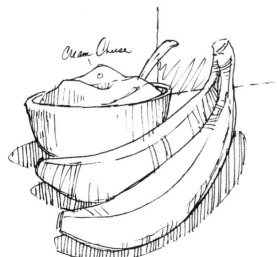

Cream Cheese

CORNELIA'S
750 W. Cornelia
Chicago, Illinois 60657
(312) 248-8333

Black Bottom Pie

4 ounces good quality
   semi-sweet chocolate
6 tablespoons unsalted butter
½ cup superfine sugar
   (not confectioners')
2 eggs, beaten
2 teaspoons vanilla, divided
1 tablespoon Cointreau

1 pie shell (8 inches), homemade
   or frozen, baked and cooled
2½ cups whipping cream
½ cup sugar
4 egg yolks
Whipped cream,
   lightly sweetened

To prepare the chocolate layer:
In the top of a double boiler, heat the chocolate, butter, and superfine sugar, stirring constantly until the chocolate is melted and the sugar is dissolved. Remove from the heat and stir in the beaten eggs, 1 teaspoon of the vanilla, and the Cointreau. Pour into the baked pie shell and cool until set.

To prepare the custard:
Preheat the oven to 325°.

Heat 2 cups of the whipping cream in a small saucepan, but do not scald. Remove from heat. Add the sugar and stir until dissolved.

In a mixing bowl, beat the egg yolks until light and pale yellow. Add the remaining ½ cup of whipping cream to the yolks slowly, stirring constantly. Then pour the yolk-cream mixture slowly into the hot cream-sugar mixture, stirring constantly. Add the remaining teaspoon of vanilla.

Pour this mixture through a strainer into a lightly greased 8-inch glass pie plate. Let set for a few minutes for the bubbles to escape.

Fill a large baking pan with 1 inch of hot water. Set the glass pie plate in this hot water bath and bake for about 45 minutes. Test the custard by inserting a knife halfway between the edge and the center. The blade should come out clean. When done, cool the custard to room temperature. Then refrigerate for several hours until cold and set.

To assemble the pie:
Run a sharp knife along the edge of the custard to loosen it from the pie plate. You may wish to set the glass pie plate in warm water for a few seconds before attempting to slide the custard out. Tilt the plate to start the custard sliding. Position it over the crust filled with the chocolate. Let the custard slide out onto the top of the chocolate layer, carefully centering the custard. Garnish with whipped cream.

Note: The chocolate layer and custard may be made a day ahead and assembled just before serving.

Serves 8.

GENESEE DEPOT
3736 N. Broadway
Chicago, Illinois 60614
(312) 528-6990

Macadamia Nut Torte

½ pound (2 sticks) unsalted butter,
 well chilled and cut into
 ½-inch bits
2¾ cups flour
3 egg yolks plus 1 extra
¾ cup sugar
¼ teaspoon vanilla

2 tablespoons heavy cream
¼ cup dark corn syrup
4 tablespoons unsalted butter
⅔ cup sugar
2 cups unsalted macadamia nuts,
 coarsely chopped

Preheat the oven to 350°.

In a large bowl, cut the chilled butter into the flour with a pastry blender until the mixture resembles coarse meal. In a separate bowl, beat 3 egg yolks with ¾ cup sugar and the vanilla until the yolks are pale yellow. Combine the egg mixture with the butter and flour to form a pliable but not sticky dough.

On a lightly floured surface, roll out the dough ¼-inch thick and cut to fit a 9-inch fluted tart pan with a removable bottom. Place the crust in the pan. Prick the bottom of the crust all over with a fork. Then line the crust with aluminum foil and place weights or dry beans on the foil. Bake in the oven for about 20 minutes or until golden brown. Remove the beans and the foil. Brush the inside of the crust with 1 beaten egg yolk and set aside to cool.

In a heavy saucepan over medium heat, combine the cream, corn syrup, 4 tablespoons of butter, and ⅔ cup sugar. Bring to a boil and cook 1 minute.

Spread the nuts in the cool tart shell. Cover with the filling and bake in a 350° oven until the filling bubbles, about 20 minutes. Cool before serving.

Serves 10 to 12.

PERIWINKLE
2511 N. Lincoln Avenue
Chicago, Illinois 60614
(312) 883-9797

Pecan and Chocolate Tart

For the pastry:
1¾ cups all-purpose flour
Pinch of salt
2 to 2½ tablespoons sugar
1¼ sticks chilled butter,
    cut into ½-inch bits
2 tablespoons chilled shortening
⅓ to ½ cup ice water

For the filling:
12 ounces pecans, whole

6 ounces semi-sweet
    chocolate, crumbled
½ cup sugar
½ cup light corn syrup
4 tablespoons unsalted
    butter, melted
2 eggs

Preheat the oven to 350°.

To prepare the pastry:
Put the flour, salt, and sugar in a food processor fitted with a steel blade. Drop the bits of butter and the chilled shortening into the machine and process for several seconds. Add ⅓ cup of the ice water to the flour-butter mixture and process again until the dough masses on the blade. Knead the dough several times to evenly distribute the butter. Form into a cake, wrap in plastic, and refrigerate for at least 2 hours before rolling.

Line a 10-inch tart pan with the pastry. Prick the bottom of the pastry with a fork. Line the pastry with foil and weight down with rice or beans. Prebake at 350° for 20 minutes. When cool, remove the foil.

To prepare the filling:
Place the pecans and chocolate, mixed, in the shell. In a mixing bowl, beat together the sugar, corn syrup, butter, and eggs. Pour this mixture on top of the chocolate and pecans. Bake at 350° for about 1 hour or until set. Cool for 20 minutes before serving.

Serves 8.

MÉLANGE
1515 N. Sheridan Road
Wilmette, Illinois 60091
(312) 256-1700

Key Lime Pie

For the pie shell:
1 1/4 cups crushed graham crackers
1/4 cup ground almonds
1/4 cup sugar
5 tablespoons melted butter

For the pie filling:
2 key limes or 4 regular limes
6 eggs, beaten
3/4 cup sugar
8 tablespoons (1 stick) butter,
      cut into tablespoon pieces

Preheat the oven to 375°.

To prepare the pie shell:
In a large bowl, combine the graham crackers, almonds, 1/4 cup sugar, and 5 tablespoons melted butter. Mix well. Pat the mixture into a 9-inch pie pan. Bake for 8 to 10 minutes. Set aside to cool.

To prepare the pie filling:
Grate the zest (green part only) from the limes. Then juice the limes. Mix the eggs with the 3/4 cup sugar, lime zest, and lime juice in a stainless steel bowl. Place the bowl over simmering water in a double boiler, whisking constantly. Cook until the mixture thickens, about 5 to 10 minutes. Watch carefully and do not overcook or the eggs will curdle.

Reduce the heat and add the 8 tablespoons of butter one piece at a time. Whisk until the butter is melted and blended. Remove the mixture from the heat and pour immediately into the cooled pie shell. Let the pie come to room temperature. Refrigerate for 6 hours or until firm to the touch.

Serves 8.

SHAW'S CRAB HOUSE
21 E. Hubbard Street
Chicago, Illinois 60611
(312) 527-2722

Key Lime Ice Cream Pie

½ cup (1 stick) unsalted butter,
   softened
1 teaspoon sugar
8 or 9 whole graham crackers,
   finely crushed
2 cans Eagle Brand
   condensed milk
2 scoops vanilla ice cream,
   softened
½ cup freshly squeezed, frozen,
   or bottled key lime juice*

To prepare the crust:
In a mixing bowl, combine the softened butter, sugar, and crushed graham crackers. Press into a 9-inch pie pan and refrigerate for 30 minutes.

To prepare the filling:
Combine the milk and the ice cream and stir with a whisk until well blended. Do not beat. Slowly pour in the key lime juice until the ingredients are blended together. Pour this mixture into the prepared graham cracker crust. Refrigerate for 6 to 8 hours before serving.

Serves 6.

*Ordinary lime juice may be substituted but the flavor will be altered slightly.

STEVIE B'S RIB CAFÉ
2623 N. Halsted
Chicago, Illinois 60614
(312) 472-7513

Frango Mint Ice Cream Pie

For the topping:
1 cup sugar
1 cup filberts, finely chopped

For the pie filling:
2 cups milk
1 cup Marshall Field's Frango mint
  chocolates

1 cup sugar
¼ teaspoon salt
1 tablespoon cornstarch
2 eggs, lightly beaten
2 cups whipping cream
1 teaspoon vanilla
2 graham cracker pie shells

To prepare the topping:
Heat the sugar in a saucepan over medium heat until it starts to dissolve. Lower the heat. Add the filberts and mix thoroughly. Transfer to a buttered cookie sheet. Spread the mixture on the cookie sheet with a knife. Cool. Remove from the cookie sheet and crush into small pieces.

To prepare the filling:
Scald 1½ cups of the milk in a saucepan. Chop the Frango mints and melt them in a double boiler. Stir the scalded milk into the chocolate. In a bowl, combine the sugar, salt, cornstarch, and the remaining ½ cup of milk. Add to the chocolate mixture. Add the eggs and cook in the double boiler until slightly thickened. Cool. Add the cream and vanilla. Freeze in an ice-cream maker according to the manufacturer's instructions. Let the ice cream soften and fill both pie shells. Sprinkle each with approximately ½ cup of the topping.

Serves 16.

THE WALNUT ROOM
Marshall Field's
111 N. State Street
Chicago, Illinois 60602
(312) 781-1000

Green Tea Ice Cream
with Fresh Raspberry Sauce

1½ pints raspberries (reserve a few
   raspberries for garnish)
1 cup sugar
1 cup water
½ quart milk
¼ ounce powdered Japanese
   green tea

8 egg yolks
¼ pound sugar
½ cup heavy cream
½ cup half-and-half

To prepare the sauce:
Place the raspberries, 1 cup sugar, and 1 cup water in a saucepan. Bring the mixture to a boil. Reduce the heat and simmer for 15 minutes, stirring occasionally to break up the raspberries. Rub the sauce through a sieve. Set aside to cool.

Note: This sauce can also be made with fresh-frozen raspberries. Because these may be sugared, add any additional sugar, if desired, to taste. No water is needed.

To prepare the ice cream:
Bring the milk to a boil in a saucepan and add the green tea. Mix together well. In a separate bowl, beat the egg yolks and sugar together until they form a ribbon. Strain this egg mixture into a saucepan. Cook over medium-high heat until just before the mixture reaches its boiling point. Then remove from the heat and let cool.

In a separate bowl, whisk the heavy cream and the half-and-half together. Pour into the egg mixture and blend well. Process in an ice-cream maker according to the manufacturer's instructions. When the ice cream is ready, pour some of the sauce onto individual chilled serving plates. Place a scoop of the ice cream on each plate and drizzle a bit of sauce over. Garnish with fresh raspberries.

Serves 15 to 20.

YOSHI'S CAFÉ
3257 N. Halsted
Chicago, Illinois 60657
(312) 248-6160

Restaurants

Index

Please send me _____ copy(ies) of **Specialties of the House** at $9.95 each. I have included $2.00 for postage and handling for the first book and $.50 for each book thereafter.

☐ Enclosed is my check or money order

☐ Please bill my ☐ VISA ☐ MASTERCARD # _____

Expires _____ Signature _____

Name _____	_____copy(ies) @ $9.95 each _____
Address _____ street	Illinois residents +
_____ city state zip	add 8% sales tax _____

SEND TO: Chicago House
      801 W. Cornelia 2-N
      Chicago, IL 60657

Shipping and
handling   + _____

TOTAL   _____

TO ORDER BY PHONE, CALL: (312) 337-0747

B-88   Expires 6/88

Please send me _____ copy(ies) of **Specialties of the House** at $9.95 each. I have included $2.00 for postage and handling for the first book and $.50 for each book thereafter.

☐ Enclosed is my check or money order

☐ Please bill my ☐ VISA ☐ MASTERCARD # _____

Expires _____ Signature _____

Name _____	_____copy(ies) @ $9.95 each _____
Address _____ street	Illinois residents +
_____ city state zip	add 8% sales tax _____

SEND TO: Chicago House
      801 W. Cornelia 2-N
      Chicago, IL 60657

Shipping and
handling   + _____

TOTAL   _____

TO ORDER BY PHONE, CALL: (312) 337-0747

B-88   Expires 6/88